I0610272

William John Loftie

A plea for art in the house with special reference to the

economy of collecting works of art

William John Loftie

A plea for art in the house with special reference to the economy of collecting works of art

ISBN/EAN: 9783337151942

Printed in Europe, USA, Canada, Australia, Japan

Cover: Foto ©Thomas Meinert / pixelio.de

More available books at **www.hansebooks.com**

A PLEA FOR

ART IN THE HOUSE,

WITH SPECIAL REFERENCE TO THE ECONOMY OF COLLECTING WORKS OF ART, AND THE IMPORTANCE OF TASTE IN EDUCATION AND MORALS.

BY

W. J. LOFTIE,

B.A., F.S.A., AUTHOR OF "IN AND OUT OF LONDON."

SECOND EDITION.

London:

MACMILLAN AND CO.

1877.

[*The Right of Translation and Reproduction is Reserved.*]

PREFACE.

THE following chapters are an attempt to put some practical rules and anecdotes into colloquial language. Almost all that has hitherto been published on Art, either at home or abroad, has been written in a manner which may almost be called poetical, so far does it differ from the plainness of what is practical. I hope I have succeeded in showing, on simple grounds, the advantages of cultivating a love for art, especially art in the family and household. I am under the persuasion that common-sense arguments may be found powerful with many people to whom high flights are unpleasant. Art is therefore pleaded for on such grounds as the manifest prudence of making collections, the civilising effects of taste upon young persons, the pleasure of pursuing an object, and, generally, the economical value of art training both to the individual, the family, and the nation at large.

A second volume of the series will be issued almost simultaneously with this one, containing some hints on " House Decoration," by Miss Rhoda Garrett and her partner, Miss Agnes Garrett.

Further volumes, by Mr. H. Stacy Marks, A.R.A., on *Drawing and Painting*, by Mrs. Oliphant, on *Dress*, by Mr. John Hullah, on *Family Music*, and by Mr. J. J. Stevenson, on *Domestic Architecture*, are in preparation ; and it is hoped that similar treatises on *Gardening*, *Sculpture and Carving*, *Needlework and Lace-making*, and other subjects connected with Art at Home, may follow in due course.

W. J. L.

CONTENTS.

b

CONTENTS.

CHAPTER IV.

CHAPTER V.

LIST OF WOODCUTS.

A PLEA FOR ART AT HOME.

CHAPTER I.

THE PRUDENCE OF COLLECTING.

FEW years ago a merchant in the west of England had in his employment a traveller who was fortunate enough to possess a taste. That such a possession may be of value I hope to show further on. This traveller's taste was for black-letter books. Wherever business took him he visited the places in which old books are to be seen and bought. Such shops are in almost every little town, and sometimes, as I have occasion to remember, they are not ostensibly book-shops; for I once bought a very scarce black-letter Bible,—a Bible of which, so far as I know, there was no example in the British Museum, or any other public collection,—and I found it among some old iron on the counter of a retired tinker at Canterbury.

LOF.   B

But this west country bagman never neglected an opportunity of picking up a little book printed before our ordinary type was in common use. He preferred little books. Very small indeed were some of them, and he gave very small prices. He knew that the early popular literature of England was often of such a character that the owner of a book might easily conceal it. In what Mr. Green calls the " English Terror," when Henry VIII. and Thomas Cromwell had set people thinking and questioning, and then hanged or burnt them for pretending to have opinions, some printers issued little books which were never licensed by the authorities : and such books are very scarce and very valuable. And this collector endeavoured wherever he could to find such books. And one day he found a prize—four prizes in fact. They were a number of Wycliffe's writings, printed in London, evidently for popular reading, but very small and curious. He bought them, as I have heard, for a shilling each ; that is, for four shillings altogether. He could find no account of them in any of the works on bibliography, and began to think they must be valuable. He had them very handsomely bound, which I dare say did not cost him more than 2*l.* so that his whole investment amounted to about 2*l.* 4*s.*

There are copies of the four little books and also of a fifth which belongs to the set, in that wonderful treasure house, the Lambeth Library : but our commercial gentleman did not know this, nor did any one else, so far as I am aware, until an event occurred, which gives me my excuse for telling this anecdote.

Our commercial traveller bethought him once, when

times were bad, as they were for so many people in 1866 and the following years, that he would sell some of the little books he had collected. So he sent a selection up to a well-known auction-room in London, and included in the parcel his four little Wycliffes.

They were duly put up and knocked down, and the four little Wycliffes fetched four hundred pounds, that is, one hundred pounds a piece.

It is easy to calculate the interest our travelling collector made on his original outlay. He spent 2*l.* 4*s.*, and kept the books two years, during which time he was out of the interest, say, at 10 per cent., or thereabouts, 5*s.* So that when his books were put up they had cost him 2*l.* 9*s.* Then the auctioneers' expenses amounted to 12½ per cent. or 50*l.* : and his whole profit was 348*l.* 2*s.* 11*d.*, or about two thousand per cent., per annum, for each of the two years.

This was, of course, an extreme example of the prudence of collecting : black-letter books are not art ; and it may be objected, that I have no right to take up time with stories not to the point. I hope to return to this question, namely, what is art, and what is not, but first I will tell another collector's story which may be a little more to the purpose.

The late Canon R. was a man of taste. When he began life he was poor, and was, I believe, chaplain to a nobleman of his own persuasion, in the country. He lived in a small house near the high road, and one day a tinker came to him with his bag of old iron, and said he had heard that Mr. R. was a collector of curiosities. Presently after much fumbling among the old iron, he brought out a bronze processional cross of the utmost beauty, made probably in the fourteenth century, and altogether such a magnificent example of the art, that poor Mr. R.'s heart beat with excitement merely at the sight of it. His practised eye showed him, as he examined it, that the bronze surface had formerly been heavily plated with silver, and in places even with gold, and the cross must have been borne before some great abbot, possibly before an archbishop.

With a trembling voice, for he had very little money, he asked the tinker how much he wanted for the cross.

" Sixpence, sir," said the man ; " and indeed I think it's quite worth it, sir—it is, I'm sure."

Canon R. thought he was dreaming.

" Sixpence," he repeated.

" Well, sir, I gave nearly that for it," said the man ; " and there's more than the weight of copper in it."

Canon R., as he told me the story, said, the mere reference to the weight of copper, and the allusion to the possibility of melting it, made him feel quite sick. He could hardly summon up strength to take out the sixpence. As soon as the tinker had it in his hand, he picked up his bag, and walked away quickly.

Canon R. looked at the cross, and could hardly believe his good fortune. Then he looked at the retreating figure of the tinker. It seemed like robbery to give him only sixpence for such a treasure. He called him back. The man came back very slowly and doubtfully.

"Look here," said Dr. R., "I think this cross is worth more than sixpence. I'll give you a shilling."

The tinker took the shilling with hesitation. He looked twice at it and twice at the priest's face. "There's summat rummy in it," was no doubt the reflection which passed through his mind. Then he took it, and again departed.

Canon R. looked at the cross, and turned to go into the house with his treasure. He told me as he took it in he felt sure it would melt away into thin air and disappear like a dream. But when he had laid it on the table, his mind was reassured, and again his conscience smote him. It was worth more than 1s. 6d. He would give the man half-a-crown,— fortunately he had half-a-crown in his pocket.

The tinker had nearly reached the gate. Canon R. called him. He stopped. "Look here, I think I have given you too little for that cross."

The man came no nearer. The Canon advanced towards him. He retreated. "I'll give you half-a-crown. Here it is," said the Canon, putting his hand into his pocket.

The tinker looked at him for a moment. Then with a look of deep suspicion, and the use of a word which sounded very like "Walker," he turned and took to his heels.

The cross has been engraved more than once, and if I do not mistake, the reader will find a very faithful representation of it as a frontispiece to Paley's *Gothic Architecture.* If this cut does not represent the same cross, it is one almost exactly like it ; and the reader can judge for himself whether it is worth half-a-crown.

Now in both these cases, that of the commercial traveller, and that of Canon R., the quality required was knowledge.

Mr. D. knew the value and scarcity of black-letter books in duodecimo. Canon R. knew the style of art practised in the fourteenth century, and could judge in a moment of the genuineness of the bronze cross.

But another and very needful quality is forethought. Some years ago, I think about forty, a young gentleman who was in a public office in London saw a pair of jars at a dealer's shop. This young gentleman had a small but sufficient allowance from his father, a country squire. The price of the jars was fifty guineas. They were of English make, I forget of what particular pottery, but I think it was Chelsea. Now fifty guineas would be very nearly a quarter's allowance, but the young man observed two things about the jars; first, that they were very beautifully painted, and secondly that the manufactory whose mark they bore had long been closed, and no more ware would issue from it. Such porcelain can never become more common, he reflected, and this is the best work that particular pottery ever produced. So he offered the dealer thirty guineas.

" No, sir, they're worth the fifty."

But fifty was more than he had to give. He went away, but came back again the next day. He offered the dealer 40*l.* and carried away his jars.

I need hardly say that his father,—when the end of the quarter came, and the son petitioned for a little advance of his allowance, at the same time telling truly what he had done—his father was shocked.

" Forty pounds for a couple of jars ! Such an extravagant son was never known." He would not have been in the very least surprised if his son had lost forty or even a hundred guineas on a horse-race, but that he should give 20*l.* a piece for a pair of jars, seemed to him simply madness.

But thirty years later that same pair of jars were sold at Christie's at a price which paid interest on the orignal outlay of 20 per cent. per annum for all the thirty years, and left a good margin over, besides, as profit.

Thus the young gentleman in the public office had put by in his youth a sum of money quite as profitably as if he had invested in shares, and he had, moreover, during thirty years of his life, enjoyed the pleasure of looking at what he considered a pair of very beautiful objects. I did not admire them when I saw them. They were ugly in shape, as I thought, and dingy in colour. But my taste in ceramics is warped, no doubt, by a strong admiration for the porcelain of China and Japan.

But the collector has another incentive. By forming a collection he does good work for the knowledge of art, and he increases the value of each individual specimen in his collection. I have spoken hitherto only of cases in which a man has bought some one object or set of objects. But collecting involves more than this. It implies what phrenologists call " comparativeness."

The collector must endeavour to ascertain the comparative excellence and rarity of the objects he collects. This is especially the case with prints.

Books, that is printed books, are much like prints in this respect. A unique book is as rare as a unique print. But every painting and every manuscript is unique ; and the collector who can afford to buy pictures and illuminations will perhaps do better than the book collector or the print collector.

On the other hand, pictures, especially good ones, are much more expensive than books. The question is which will afford the collector the greatest measure of enjoyment. Some men like one thing and some another ; but unquestionably the man who wishes to make his house look nice, and who wants his family and his friends to partake of his enjoyment, will prefer pictures or prints, which can be hung on his walls, to anything else.

But the cheapest collection that can be made is one of books. The experienced buyer lays out very little money. If he has gathered a library judiciously he can sell it at a large profit : for example :—

A man of moderate means made a study of a certain class of religious books. They were rare, and often they were beautifully illustrated with cuts and engravings. When he had collected a hundred or more, one by one, and at very low prices, he began to find he knew more about them than anybody else ; he could, therefore, confidently bid for a book, knowing perhaps that it was perfect, perhaps that it was unique, and could exercise a little discrimination. Every now and then he picked up a treasure, and his knowledge grew rapidly. For instance, one day he saw a large volume, which he knew to be rare, put up at a sale. It fetched what seemed a good price, 4*l*., I think.   He went home, not having bought it; but his interest being aroused by finding he knew very little of that particular edition, he tried to discover more.   After some research he found it was extremely scarce.   No other copy had ever occurred for sale.   It had been rigidly suppressed. So, full of excitement, he rushed to the saleroom to discover the name of the buyer, determining to offer him a profit on his purchase.

The clerk informed him of the name, but added that the book was found to have a worm-hole and had been returned—in other words, the buyer, a bookseller, thought his bargain too dear.   Our young collector asked when it would be re-sold.

"In about a month," was the reply; "you shall have notice."

A month elapsed, and then another, but at last the precious volume came up again for sale.

Unfortunately for our friend, he was not his own master.   Duty called him away on the long expected day.   He found it would be impossible for him to go to the sale.

He went in his despair to a man on whom he could depend, and said to him, "Buy me that book at a moderate price.   It may fetch four or five guineas, perhaps more,—but I would go to 10*l*. and even a few shillings more, if there is any chance of getting it."

All day he thought of the book.   Had he offered enough ?   Had he offered too much ?   Could he have made any mistake about it ?   Would his man be punctual ?   In short he was full of contradictory questions, and almost trembling with excitement.

The next morning came. He went to the saleroom, almost afraid to ask about the book. He had not been able to see his agent, and came to ask the clerk.

" What was the number of the lot, sir ? "

" It was No. so-and-so."

The clerk looked it out slowly. My friend felt as if it took hours to find the entry.

" I find, sir," said the clerk, at length, " that the lot 's entered to your name at four-and-sixpence."

When he had gathered about two hundred volumes he made an elaborate catalogue. It was much noticed and reviewed. The subject was of some interest to the general public ; and my friend's book, a mere list, was bought by many people who did not care for bibliography. Its publication, however, cut off his sources of supply. Every bookseller could now judge as well as himself, of the value and rarity of books of this class. He determined to sell his collection.

So he had a list printed, and sent it to people who were likely to buy, and meanwhile he prepared to sell by auction, if necessary. But in a few weeks he had an offer from a great public library, which he accepted. It was that he should send them all the books in his list, and that the trustees of the library, on condition of his taking a certain sum, would keep the collection together and put them in a bookcase inscribed with his name.

He could not afford to present them, though he would willingly have done so, but this offer seemed to him so pleasing that he accepted it, and sent the books.

As I happened to hear both the sum laid out and the sum received, and as this chapter is not so much on the art or ethics, as on the prudence, of collecting, I may as well give them as nearly as I can remember. He had laid out altogether on buying and on binding 78*l.* This outlay had been spread over some three or four years. He received 225*l.*, of which the odd 25*l.* was absorbed by various expenses connected with the printing and packing. His profit was thus 122*l.*

I say nothing of the pleasure he had taken in the pursuit, nor yet of the advantages of the knowledge he acquired, and the many incidental benefits which accrued to him.

The point on which I am anxious to insist is merely that it is often profitable to collect judiciously. I think this point may be taken as proved. I have purposely avoided, for the present, any mention of the great collections of which one so constantly hears. I only speak of what may be done in a very small way by a man engaged in some other business and only collecting in his leisure hours, and with what may be called his leisure money.

People who live in great cities are often shocked to find how much is spent without any return. Pocket money makes away with itself and leaves no mark behind. You have bought nothing yet your money is gone. We cannot all bring ourselves to the state of mind of a late nobleman, who having several hundreds of thousands a year used to go out without any money in his purse for fear he should be induced by pity or a passing fancy to spend even sixpence. Without going this length, we might yet find it possible to

economise considerably in this one particular. The
man is singular who does not enjoy buying, just as
the sportsman enjoys killing, for its own sake. We
must buy, and there are few pleasures more to be
enjoyed, and few also which need cost us so little, and
which may be more innocent. For though it may
seems a little paradoxical to say that spending
money, even judiciously, is a cheap pleasure, I will
endeavour to prove the truth of the proposition.

There are two pleasures in buying. One is in the
act of buying itself, the other in the subsequent possession of the object bought. But if the object be one
which soon loses its value this second pleasure is gone
with it. A young man likes to go to an arcade and
spend his money in gorgeous jewellery, satin neck-
cloths, and other things which may safely be summed
up in the single word " toys." The pleasure of buying
these things, that is of choosing them, must be considerable, for many young men of wealth seem to do
nothing else, and it would be hard to believe that
they do it from any sense of duty, and not rather from
self-gratification. But that the choice is not of a kind
to give the æsthetic faculties much play is also evident
Though the buyer lavishes both time and money on
diamonds and cigars, his taste is often not sufficient
to enable him to give any reason for his preferences.
The fancy shops are furnished to reach him, and they
succeed, for as he has no taste, in the true sense of
the word,—one which implies something of reflection
—he is guided wholly by his fancy. Novelty, therefore, is the first thing he seeks. It requires no mental
effort to know that you never saw a thing before, or

do not recollect it, which comes to the same thing. As your experience increases you begin to find that real novelty is very rare, and that for the most part you have been imposed on. But by this time you have also found that few of the things for which you paid such long prices are worth anything now, and you are disgusted to see that though your money is gone you have nothing to show for it.

This kind of expenditure, then, is not remunerative. And there is another kind, which is also, as a rule, a loss of money.

You may buy with taste but without knowledge. Thus a few years ago a young man who had considerable command of money, and also considerable taste for art, took the advice of a well-known print-seller, who is still alive, and whom therefore I refrain from mentioning by name. This man advised him to buy the large engravings from Landseer's pictures, and offered him proofs at very high prices, telling him that in a very few years they would be worth twice as much. After a time our young friend married.

"Now," he said, "I will realize all that money I put into engravings ; they should be worth a great sum by this time." He went accordingly to the dealer. What was his surprise to hear they were only worth twice as many shillings as he had given pounds !

At first he said he would bring an action against the printseller. But after a time he grew more composed, as he saw that the fault was his own, and was this :—He had bought without knowledge. He was content with, say, the last proof; and everyone knows that the first ordinary print is almost as good as the last proof, and frequently even better. My friend had thought any proof was equal to any other proof from the same plate, and he had made the further mistake of allowing the dealer to choose for him, without any mental exercise on his own part.

But I have only shown that buying novelties and buying good things without knowledge are not cheap pleasures. I have still to show how it may be cheap to buy.

The late Mr. Gillott, of Birmingham, began as soon as he had the money to buy a picture or two every year from some rising artist. I am told that he trusted his own judgment. This implies that he had judgment to trust. He enjoyed the possession of the pictures very much. They were a constant source of intense pleasure to him. He was an illiterate man, having raised himself from the lowest condition. I do not know whether he could read. He certainly could not read so as to be fond of reading, and his great resource was in his picture gallery. When he died I went to Birmingham to see it before it should be dispersed; and I afterwards attended the famous sale at Christie's. I may have more to say about it presently. My present purpose is only to show that Mr. Gillott's gallery was a cheap pleasure. The fact is it cost nothing. When it was dispersed there were not wanting people to assert that the increase in the value of the pictures since they were painted was such as to bring in to Mr. Gillott's heirs a sum equal to the aggregate produce at 20 per cent.

per annum of all the money spent. And it is curious further to observe, that the pictures which Mr. Gillott had bought at the highest prices fetched less at his sale than those he had given the least money for. The Ettys, the Maclises, the Wilsons, which formed, as he probably thought, the great features of his gallery, fetched nothing in comparison with the Turner water-colours, and the Müllers, for which comparatively he had given very little.

But let us take a less prominent case, as more illustrative of the position, that collecting may be a cheap pleasure. A man with a taste for early printed books, and with a knowledge of the history of the art, goes into an auction room or a bookseller's every now and then as he passes by on his daily road to business. Sometimes he sees a rare book going for a low price, and he buys it. More often he has to be content while others buy who are wealthier, but he learns something regarding the comparative value and rarity of particular books. He derives a vast amount of enjoyment from his pursuit. He meets intellectual men on common ground. He has a little wholesome excitement now and then at a sale. And he has the quiet pleasure of collating his treasures of an evening, of mending them, of binding them, perhaps of making one perfect whole from several fragments. He learns a great deal, and that too of a useful kind, and though he often has to walk or go in the omnibus rather than take a cab, he does not mind it. The taste, the consciousness that he has something behind the daily routine of business life, is worth much to him, and meanwhile he is steadily gathering a collection. All

those cab drives he does not take, all those newspapers
and magazines he does not buy, all those cigars he
does not smoke, all those club luncheons he does not
eat, all those coats, hats, hosen, and other garments
he does as well without, have gone to increase the
collection. Had he bought all these things he would
have none of them to leave ; but the mere chips and
parings of ordinary life have given him enough to
form a good, if a small, collection, and at his death, or
before it, they are sold for such a sum as will materially
add to the resources of his family.

This is the kind of case on which I would rather
dwell ; and indeed the object of my present book is
to show that a very small expenditure on worthy
objects of art is both good and pleasant in itself,
and also a prudent piece of economy.

I will take one more example. The facts of it are
true, but one or two particulars, of no importance to
the matter in hand, are varied, as many of the actors
in the story are still alive.

About forty years ago, let us say, but it may have
been fifty, and it may have been ten, a country baronet
of moderate wealth married for the second time. His
only son did not get on with his stepmother. He was
wild, and would not be restrained. She had a large
family in the course of time ; and the stepson, having
gone on from bad to worse, died in miserable circumstances, into which we need not pry further than to
say that, immediately after his death, the old baronet
had a letter acquainting him with the fact that his son
had married just before his death, and that the widow
hoped shortly to present him with a grandchild.

Knowing, as he too well did, the kind of female company into which his prodigal son habitually entered, the old man was terribly shocked at the news. His second wife's eldest boy was a good lad, and was likely to be a comfort to himself and a credit to his family. But if this woman should have a son then all would go into her control, and the result probably would be the utter ruin of his ancient family.

So much did these apprehensions distress him that he died a very few months after his eldest son. Almost at the same time the widow wrote to say she was the mother of a boy.

The consternation in the family may be imagined. The young mother had taken care to provide for all possible contingencies. There were witnesses to the marriage and to everything. And though the witnesses chiefly belonged to the same class as the lady herself, their testimony was not thereby invalidated.

At first the young uncle and his mother endeavoured to do what they could to draw the heir and his mother to them, and, promising to forget all past errors, offered to receive her into the family, and to make no opposition to the child's succession. But before very long curious rumours reached them. They made inquiries, which were attended with great expense, and led to nothing. By degrees, however, one little circumstance after another accumulated till they were able to take a decisive step. They boldly challenged the paternity of the child, and refused to acknowledge it or its mother.

Legal proof was still difficult to obtain. It was
LOF.   C

obtained at last, however, and by a mere accident. The child was proved to be the offspring of a washerwoman at Stepney; and though the marriage was never called in question, it is said that the witnesses to it were no more to be believed than those who testified to the birth of the false heir.

A more romantic story has seldom been told in our law-courts. The general public were greatly entertained. But the bill had to be paid, and of that the public knew nothing. A great deal of money had been spent or was owed, and the new baronet's success seemed to have been purchased at a cost which would keep him poor all his life.

But it so happened that shortly after these events a man of taste, who was well acquainted with certain branches of art and archæology, was staying in the house. And one day the unfortunate young heir showed him a great boxful of old curiosities—coins, let us say; they were not coins, but coins will do for my purpose. "They were gathered by my great-grandfather, and are of all ages and kinds. Do you think they would be worth selling? They did not cost much, for my ancestor never had much money to spend."

The connoisseur looked over them for a few minutes. There were a great number, most of them worthless. But presently he jumped up with an exclamation: "This must be a forgery," he cried. "The only known example is in the Museum; they gave a thousand pounds for it, and it should be worth more now."

He had two or three more surprises, and finally determined to take the whole boxful to town, and show them to an expert.

When the box of coins had been thoroughly ransacked, about four hundred were found to be of great value. Of these two hundred were at once bought for a great public collection at an immense price, as it seemed to their owner ; and the rest were sent to a saleroom. There they brought such a sum as, added to that obtained from the museum, paid off all the costs of the lawsuit, and enabled the young baronet to start in life out of debt from that cause at least.

From which may be drawn the safe moral that, if you collect what may seem common enough now, a few years hence your grandchildren may have cause to bless you. How far it is to be considered worth while to make a collection in order to deserve the thanks of posterity I cannot say, but I can promise you a great deal of pleasure for yourself from the pursuit, and I think I may venture to claim that I have made out some part of my original proposition—that spending money in this way is a cheap enjoyment.

It may of course be objected that collecting is not in itself the practice of art. But, except for people who are actually artists, much that goes to make home beautiful must of necessity be obtained by judicious collecting. It might easily be proved that articles which are really beautiful owe their chief attraction to the sense of suitability and permanent value which is required to make them satisfactory.

C 2

But, further than this, it may fairly be argued, and, indeed, has several times been pointed out already, that it is the duty of every one who is so fortunate as to possess a home and to be the head of a family, to endeavour, so far as he can, to make his family happy by making his home beautiful.

CHAPTER II.

FURNISHING AND OLD FURNITURE.

EVEN economical collecting is open to a certain suspicion. Too many men collect only for their own private gratification; and it may be as well before we go further to draw a sharp line between the man who gathers objects in which he alone is interested, and the man who desires to beautify his house with what he buys. My concern here is with the latter only. The old Adam in me may perhaps make me lenient to the faults of the other class, but Art at Home is art calculated to give pleasure to as many as possible in the home, and to make its rooms as pretty and attractive as possible. The bibliomaniac too often forgets others in his comparatively solitary pursuit, and the collector of autographs can have but little regard for the pleasures of his family. If things are only bought to be stowed away in portfolios and cupboards, they are merely money laid by to accumulate.

But this is not the ideal of collecting which I wish

to inculcate.   If, as we proceed, we keep before our eyes the thought that whatever is brought into the house should go towards the decoration, or at least the beauty of the house, we shall see that it is quite easy to add that nothing should be brought in which is without a permanent value.

Collecting, indeed, is only one name for the thing. I do not want to see everybody collecting.   I do not admire private museums.   I think houses which are ugly and badly furnished and uncomfortable, are none the better for being filled with curiosities.   But short of this there is something to be done.   I go into my neighbour Brown's house, and this is what I see :— ·

The carpet is modern " Brussels ; " the curtains are figured " rep ; " the hall and passages are covered with oil-cloths ; the furniture is of the last new pattern, designed in the " Gothic style," by Messrs Oak and Velvet, upholsterers and undertakers.   Brown tells me complacently that he has spent a thousand pounds on furnishing the sitting-rooms, and asks me to look at the frames of his prints.

They are gorgeous enough, certainly.   " Now," says Brown, " I venture to say you can hardly tell them from carved and gilt wood.   They are done by a new process."

You look at the prints for which the imitation frames were procured.   They are late pale impressions of poor second-rate works, of which even proofs would be worthless, but Brown has had to pay some cheating dealer a good sum for them.   It is the same with everything.   Its only possible value, at the best, was in its novelty.   A year's wear makes it worthless.

These dining-room chairs are of carved oak, "carved by machinery" of course, and the backs are marked with Brown's monogram in gilding on the scarlet leather. They have cost him between two and three guineas apiece, and he is naturally proud of them But what are they worth? What is anything in the house worth? Well, at most, a third of the price he has paid.

Take the chairs as an example, Say they cost Brown 2*l.* 10*s.* each. They are carved by machinery, and are of the latest pattern. But since he bought them, a newer and still more attractive pattern has come out, and so their value as being in the fashion is gone; and their carving, too, is rather a drawback, for the carvers have invented a new way of doing such work, and can turn it out so cheaply, that chairs twice as fine as Brown's are to be had for 25*s.*

It is the same with prints and their frames. The prints never were worth anything, and the frames, after a year's hanging on the walls, have the new look well rubbed off, and are not worth doing up a second time.

It would be useless to go through all the items. But if Brown's things are sold they may perhaps fetch 300*l.* perhaps 400*l.* So that he has paid 600*l.* for his use of them, and if he has them long he will lose still more.

Now I go into, say, Smith's house. Smith is a poorer man than Brown, but now and then he has what he calls a windfall : so that on the whole he has in the course of a number of years spent about as much on his drawing-rooms, study, and dining-room as Brown on his.

When he and Mrs. Smith went into residence, there
was very little furniture in the house.   They dined on
a small, deal table, and had no sideboard.   Their dinner
chairs had cane seats.   But there was a very pretty
old Turkey carpet on the floor.   " I was looking out
for a carpet like that," said Smith, " for years.   They
are not made now.   See how beautiful is the contrast
of bright blue and scarlet, with black to quiet them.
Nowadays they are magenta and dark blue, and I
prefer to do without a carpet rather than have to look
every day at anything so discordant.   Now this one
was made a hundred years ago, I dare say.   It is not
the better for that, but it has been all the time in an
old country house, and it is not much the worse.
Money would not buy such a Turkey at a shop, and
I picked it up cheap enough, by looking after it
myself."

When I go to Smith's again at an interval of a few
months, I find he has managed to acquire a sideboard.
It is a chest or large cupboard of oak, beautifully
carved.

"Now," he cries in triumph, "you thought me an
ass to have no sideboard.   But I knew better.   Ten
years ago I happened to be at a furniture sale, and I
saw that very same cupboard knocked down for a
small sum, but failed to catch the buyer's name.   I
did not want a sideboard then, nor for a long time
after, but one day on going through a Wardour Street
warehouse—only not in Wardour Street, you know,—
I saw my old friend.   I said nothing then.   But when
I came here I went to ask for it.   ' It's gone to a gent
in the country,' said the dealer.   So I asked no more,

but felt very sorry I had not secured it.   After waiting some months, and seeing nothing I liked to go with my Turkey, I went and asked the dealer if he had any pieces out of which I could make up a jury sideboard for the time being.   He said he had an old chest without any back or any feet, which he was going to break· up and put into other pieces of furniture. 'Is it old?' I asked. 'As old as Methusalem,' he answered. 'Is it pretty?' I asked again. 'Was be-ootiful,' he answered, 'but werry dilapidated.' 'Let me see it,' said I.   So he took me up to the topmost story of his house, to a little back room.   I recognized the place, and the outside of the door as that of the room in which my lamented cupboard had once stood.   Could it be there still, after all? thought I. I actually felt my heart beating under my waistcoat.   He opened the door.   There was my old friend, dilapidated as he had said, but the carving whole, and all this lovely frieze, and the heads of these Corinthian pillars, and above all the date—only look at that! 1632—and it looks a hundred years later, so fine is the carving!   'Well,' I said, trembling, 'what do you want for that?'   'I'll take half a dozen guineas, if you'll spend a couple more in doin' of it up at my shop.'   I jumped at the bargain, only for appearance' sake, offering him pounds instead of guineas. I do not think," continued Smith, with hesitation, " I do not think he saw the date on it.   You cannot see it till you look for it, but what's the good of my having the use of my eyes, and ever so many years' practice if I can't get a bargain now and then?"

Smith's sideboard is represented in the frontispiece,

and his house is, after a few years, becoming very pretty. He has two or three pictures, for instance, bought at long intervals. "Who is that?" I ask him, "an ancestor, I suppose; it looks like a Reynolds."

"It is a Reynolds," he replies with complacency.

It would be rude to make any further remarks; but I cannot help wondering how Smith comes to have a Reynolds worth, say, 250*l*.

"An ancestor?" I repeat.

"Not at all," he replies. "My illustrious ancestors, 'stirps preclarorum Smithorum' as a monument in the Abbey puts it, never could have afforded to sit to Reynolds. He would have asked a long price for such a portrait as that; and it's worth more now. I bought it "——

Of course he told me all about it; whom it represented, what he gave; what he had been offered for it since; and so on.

Then Smith has a very nice pair of tapestry *portières* for curtains, and his chandelier is of wrought brass, and a little china is in a cabinet in the drawing-room, and I observe everywhere, with a certain economy, a distinct effort to have everything of the best, ancient or modern; and I know that if anything should happen to Smith, he will leave something behind. He says himself with truth,

"I have been three years furnishing. I have paid for all—drawing-rooms and bedrooms—as nearly as possible 1000*l*., and now the babies are multiplying and I must stop buying, but it is a satisfaction to think that what I have will sell for as much as I gave, or

more, even after a few years' wear; and that it is
pretty to look at and pleasant to live in the house
with; and that moreover I have had a lot of fun
buying it.

"In fact," he concludes, "buying things that are
pretty and good, is the only way I know by which
you can both eat your cake and have it too."

Smith is undoubtedly right, and if any one will
compare his house with Brown's after a few years are
past, he will see the advantage of Smith's method.

We live so much with our furniture that it seems
to me very odd that we care so little about its look.
We have, many of us, got a false idea that pretty
things cost more than ugly ones. There cannot be a
greater mistake, but we make it very easily. If we
go into an ordinary furniture shop we find the price
depends almost solely on the amount of ornament.
But ornament is not beauty in itself. An old Greek
vase, used for carrying water from the well, without
any ornament or pattern on it of any kind is more
beautiful to look at than anything we can make now:
and it is the same with furniture. We want chairs, for
example, not to have monograms on the backs where
we have no eyes to correspond, but to be solid under
us, and to give us the idea when we sit down that we
can never get to the bottom of the springs.

The permanent things in the room should carry the
ornament. The best ornament the chairs and sofas
can have is good upholstery, and a look of comfort.
But a cabinet against the wall may be as ornate as
you please, if it is not more ornate than what it
contains. It is ridiculous to see a gorgeous buhl

cupboard, with glass doors, and covered all over with tortoiseshell and ormolu, yet only containing Bohemian glass, Swiss cottages, and the leaning tower of Pisa in alabaster.

This incongruity is very unpleasing and the most common of all forms of household discord. I have seen a room decorated in the Louis Quatorze style and filled with Gothic furniture. And I have seen an ancient and beautiful "oak parlour" in a manorhouse with a Wardour Street chimney-piece, and a German transparency in the window.

It is however, impossible in furnishing to avoid incongruity altogether, and all we can do in order to counteract its effects is to avoid extremes.

It was the fashion some years ago, with many people to go in for things in a style invented by the late Mr. Pugin and by him called "Perpendicular." They were for the most part applications of the architectural principles of the 15th century to chairs and tables. The most familiar examples of this system of treatment are to be seen in the committee rooms of the Houses of Parliament at Westminster.

Now furniture in this style has the singular property of looking bad itself with furniture in any other style and also of injuring the appearance of whatever is placed with it. This is simply because it is an extreme style. I do not believe they really used furniture like it when the perpendicular houses and churches were first built. As a matter of fact hardly any examples of that period have come down to us. The few that we see which look like it are not really " perpendicular," being the work of the French, Flemish

or German schools, and they look just as bad with the
real thing as if they were Grecian.

I do not want to disparage Gothic furniture.   Much
of it is very beautiful, especially when the carving is
worthy of the style; but I want, in passing, to notice
it as a typical extreme; and I do so for this reason :
the best periods of domestic furniture are not Gothic ;
so, if you have beautiful furniture, it is almost a
necessity to have it of a very different character from
Pugin Gothic, and the result is unpleasant.

It is only millionaires who can hope to have so
much genuine old Gothic furniture as to make it possible to furnish a room, much less a house.   But the
case is different with a later style.   The Queen Anne
style, of which people talk so much now, is a very
good one for furniture.   The best specimens come from
Holland, where the operation of the Code Napoleon
is breaking up the great old families ; beautiful examples of inlaid work are to be had at a moderate
cost, and harmonise very well with modern furniture
in any style except " Pugin."   This is not the place
to go into particulars as to design in furniture ; the
Misses Garrett have discussed the whole subject in
their little manual of *House Decoration,* which
forms the second volume of this series : but the principles of selection may be briefly laid down, as
depending on comfort, durability, and beauty.

The first thing to think of in choosing furniture is
comfort.   If you want chairs for a dining-room your
object will be to find chairs on which a man may sit
to eat at table without being obliged to lean forward
too much, without finding himself so far elevated that

he cannot touch the ground with his feet, and without backs so carved that after dinner he is in a hurry to remove to the sofa. Comfort in the dining-room is very different from comfort in the drawing-room. It is usual to have a number of little light chairs which have only one merit, namely, that they are easily moved about. But a comfortable drawing-room should have plenty of low arm-chairs on good easy running casters, with a sofa or two, all covered with some material on which one need not be afraid to sit. There should be no central table, but, as at a club, there should be a number of small but firm tea-tables on which you may safely place your lamp or your cup and saucer. A fender stool is a comfortable addition in winter, and there should be little brackets by the fireside where you may lay down a book or a cup.

As to durability, it will be found a source of economy. I once saw a gentleman sit down on one of the flimsy spider chairs of which I have spoken, and when he leaned back, the whole back of the chair broke away, and not only gave him a dangerous fall, but cut a large piece out of his new coat. But a strong well upholstered chair with very little woodwork visible will last a long time and may be repeatedly re-covered.

When you have obtained a chair or a sofa which is both strong and comfortable, you will find, perhaps with surprise, that the beauty has come of itself. A comfortable chair looks pretty on account of its evident fitness for the place it occupies, while an uncomfortable chair let it be never so finely carved, is ugly because it produces in the seer, an unpleasing sense of the unhappiness of sitting in it.

So far I have spoken chiefly of chairs. But there are many things in which taste is more necessary. Cabinets and bookcases, for example, being often made very gorgeous, not to say, ornamental, are calculated to challenge observation, and should be chosen with care. But the same principles will apply to them as to tables and chairs. Fitness for their employment and strength will generally ensure a certain amount of beauty ; the ornament may be added under certain restrictions. It must be remembered that ornament is not in itself necessarily beautiful. Too often a handsome, strong, well-arranged bookcase is ruined in appearance by useless and meaningless ornament. Books are the best ornament of the bookcase, and if you have a bookcase covered with ornament you cannot without violating harmony put shabbily bound books into it. The same principle applies to cabinets, as I remarked above. If you have curiosities, which are not works of art, to display, you must be very careful not to turn your room into a museum. But if you have beautiful china, or ivories, or anything else of the kind, you will find that a very magnificently ornamented cabinet may sometimes be used with advantage. But on the whole I think it will be found that the plain brass and glass cabinets for the display of china, which are preferred by the great collectors are really the prettiest as well as the best. Sometimes, it is true, a piece of beautiful carving or inlay may be worth having as a cabinet for its own sake. A fine specimen of Indian lacquer, or ebony and ivory, cr marqueterie is often a great set off to a drawing-room. One good thing of the kind will, so to speak, furnish the apartment. The great difficulty is to know what to put into it, and the selector will find, as a rule, that when he buys anything of this kind he had better choose, if it is a cupboard or cabinet, one with close doors than one with a glass front. The glass front is more attractive at first sight, but a fine cabinet filled with shabby books, or with things packed away and looking as if they were in a shop greatly mars the effect of a room.

In choosing things of this kind, therefore, a few general principles may easily be laid down. It is better to have your drawing-room cabinets too plain than too ornamental, unless the ornament is of the very best and highest character. And again, it is better to have one thing of first-rate quality, and everything else of the utmost plainness, than to have a mixture of styles and degrees, and to have one thing good, another poor, and a third, perhaps, imitation.

Nor can I leave this subject without a few words as to imitations in general. A very prominent and re-markable example occurs to me. A late eminent collector of fine furniture left among other valuable things some Louis Quatorze tables inlaid and mounted in bronze and ormolu. They had cost him fabulous sums, yet at his famous sale, two years ago, they fetched very moderate prices.

Everyone was surprised who knew their beauty, except those who knew further that their late owner had been at great pains and expense to have a table, or some tables, made in exact imitation of old work.

He had succeeded so well that it was found impossible after his death to know the copy from the original, and both suffered in consequence. I have heard that for a pair of such tables his expenses were as follows: the original Louis Quatorze, price 250*l.* ; the copy, 350*l.*, or thereabouts, thus making the two cost no less than 600*l.* Considering the increase in value of such articles, the genuine table should have fetched almost that sum alone, and the new one a price at least equal to its cost. But one fetched less than 200*l.*, and the other, which some judges pronounced to be the original, about 230*l.*

The lesson to be drawn from this is that the market for objects of taste is extremely sensitive, and that, though one article may be just as good as another, tables may have a character to lose like men and women, and should be absolutely above suspicion. Everything in the sale was affected by the doubts thrown on these tables, and everything suffered accordingly.

In furnishing handsomely, therefore, it will be better to buy either genuine old things or good new things, and to avoid new things which profess to be in the style of something old. Good, durable, solid furniture in the best style of the day will always be valuable, and for the most part it may safely be said that genuine work, if it is pleasing to the eye and commodious, will always command a good price.

So much then for tables and chairs. The dweller in the modern house suffers more from a slighter cause. There are few things which give the sensitive eye more pain than ugly curtains, covers, wall-papers, and carpets ; and few, on the other hand, which will allow of more artistic, harmonious, and satisfactory treatment.

A few years ago chintzes were made of startlingly brilliant colours, and covered with large flowers, sometimes natural and sometimes of the kind known to tradesmen as " exotic." They were often very handsome, and in days when four-post beds were in common use and iron beds were only known in legends of Procrustes and of Og, the King of Bashan, they formed appropriate hangings, and looked better with old oak or well-turned mahogany than anything else.

But of late we have been taught that the patterns on curtains and walls should always be flat, that is, unshaded ; and our fine old chintzes have been discarded, and wretched little spotty things substituted. No doubt, as a matter of principle, patterns should be flat. But the flatness of a modern speckled calico and the flatness of a Turkey or a Persian carpet are two very different things.

In choosing chintzes and calicoes for curtains, then, it may be necessary to remember that shaded patterns must be very handsome and contain a great many colours to be at all endurable, and that the modern patterns are more easily harmonized with other furniture and with wall-papers. The rules for the form of the patterns, again, will be that a large pattern makes a little room look still more little, and that a perpendicular stripe tends to lower the appearance of height. So that if your ceiling or your window is low you will avoid a stripe lest you should make it look lower even than it is, and if your room is small you will adapt the pattern to it, so as, by multiplying the parts, to increase the appearance of size.

In sitting-rooms it is usual to have net curtains in summer, and to use some woollen material in the winter. Sometimes the "rep" and the net hang together. Net curtains with large patterns of ferns, flowers, trees, and other pictures on them are extremely ugly as a rule. The material has no relation to the picture, which is an imperfect one at the best, and the forms are often exceedingly ungraceful. The prettiest lace curtains are covered with a simple diaper or spot, such as a cross or a fleur-de-lis, but too often the border is of a different character from the main pattern, and both are in consequence spoilt.

The woollen materials, or "reps," are also often very ugly from the bad taste of the patterns on them. But if we had the courage to use them, we should probably find they were better without any pattern. A plain rep curtain with a border at the bottom may be made to look very well. And at a very moderate expense it is very possible to turn such curtains into a very decorative feature of the drawing-room furniture. I have seen them treated in various ways with success. For instance, in an old house in the country I have seen the pair of curtains each almost covered with an *appliqué* figure in coarse canvas, of one of the family supporters. We are not all privileged to bear supporters, but any heraldic animal might be employed with success, as, for example, the lions are placed on the mantle of Lady Tiptoft in the well-known brass at Enfield. But a simpler ornament may be made by sewing tape of some suitable colour on the curtains in transverse lines, six inches or so apart, and placing a motto in large twisted letters, also made of tape, between the lines. This sort of treatment admits of endless variety, and circles containing monograms or coats of arms may be placed on the centre of the curtain. But all such devices involve a considerable amount of trouble and some knowledge, and if they cannot be done at home it is better not to attempt them, as furniture tradesmen make it a rule to over-charge their customers for anything the least out of the common, and seldom carry out such an order with real taste.

But rules for the country will not apply in town, where smoke spoils everything of the nature of drapery, and where all colours are soon reduced to the same dingy brown. In town, therefore, it is better to have a succession of curtains which can be taken down and sent to the dyers to be cleaned at short intervals. Beauty in such things must be sub-servient to cleanliness, and the prettiest pattern is that one which will take the least dirt and bear cleaning best.

It is the same with wall-paper. In bedrooms in town nothing is so pleasant as a paper without any pattern and well covered with varnish. At short intervals it can be washed down with soap and water, and is wholesome as well as pretty. But in the country the pattern on the bedroom walls is a matter of importance, and great diversities of opinion exist as to shaded patterns, natural flowers, spots, stripes, and grounds. The fact is, no absolute rule can be laid down. I have seen a pretty sunny room covered with paper which violated every rule. It represented a trellis work with roses peeping through, and looked exceedingly well, as roses grew on the outside of the window, and looked in at their own portraits. In the country, too, it is possible to have what is absolutely forbidden in town, that is, a white ground : and the only rule I should care to lay down would be this, that the smaller the room the less prominent should the pattern be.

In sitting-rooms the paper is always a serious sub-ject. I like to see dining-rooms painted or panelled, especially in town, but the drawing-room, according to all received traditions, must be papered ; and nothing can be more hideous than the majority of the London drawing-room wall-papers. It is melancholy to see the helplessness of a couple who go to choose among a number of patterns in a book. All the pattern pieces are of the same size, so that it is ab-solutely impossible to compare a large one with a small one, and we are surprised to find when the paper is hung that it looks quite different from what we expected.

In a woodcut on the next page will be seen an example of how a drawing-room may be papered with-out any pattern. The room is small, being only some twenty feet by eighteen, but it is high for its size. The paper is of a cool grey, all over, a tint between blue and slate colour. When it was hung the tenant of the house. enlisted the services of what is called a "writer," a painter of names over shop doors, who, under his direction, painted at intervals of a few feet

a series of mottoes in black, in Old English characters. These inscriptions were sloped diagonally, "per bend," as heralds say, and the black looked well on the grey; between the lines a few little shields were stencilled. At the opposite side of the room, over the fire-place, was a line from the book of Job, old version, "Man is born unto travail as the sparks fly upward," at the top of the projection of the chimney, and the sloping mottoes were continued wherever there was sufficient space, a different slope being adopted, to avoid uniformity of effect.

This arrangement would have been impossible had there been a pattern on the paper, and it is easy to understand that a plain paper, absolutely without a pattern, would be better than one with an ugly or an unsuitable pattern. It is not easy to make up one's mind to do without the pattern, but after a little education a man's eye becomes as sensitive as his ear, and he prefers plainness to offensive ugliness, just as he prefers silence to the sound of a barrel organ.

In London and some other northern capitals it is necessary to " remember the blacks." I am not going to say anything about the Slave Trade. But when we are arranging the decorations of our rooms we must make all our calculations with a distinct reservation. Nothing must come in but what can be easily cleaned. I know a house in which the owner, a French lady, had her drawing-room " done up " in the Parisian style. There was a pretty bright Aubusson carpet with a white ground, a magnificent bunch of flowers, and a broad border. The carpet only covered the centre of the floor, and the edges were waxed.

The walls and doors had looking-glasses let into them framed in fantastic gilt mouldings. The general effect at first was very pleasant.

But when a year was past a more deplorable spectacle can hardly be imagined. Had the room been very plain one might not have perceived its change. But everywhere the eye was offended, assaulted, I may say, by faded flowers, blackened mouldings, layers of soot, tarnished gilding, filthy curtains, the floors sticky with a kind of black mud, the sprightly carpet the colour of yellow blotting paper after a week's use, and a general air of poverty and dirt, scarcely imaginable. The housemaid could not clean the mouldings, the waxed floor caught the " blacks,' the gas soon left its shadow on the painted ceiling, and an army of servants could not have rescued that unfortunate room.

Just as bright and as pleasant a room, but with a brightness which will last was shown me lately. The floors were stained and strongly varnished, so that they could be as easily washed as a tile pavement, and would not imbibe any dampness. A Persian carpet with a black ground was in the centre. Round the walls up to the height of the lock of the door was a framing of slightly chamfered wooden panels painted maroon, and behind it, kept close to the wall by the framing, was some thin Japanese or Indian matting, without pattern, of a dark cream colour ; by unscrewing the panelling it was easy at any time to change or turn the hangings. Above the panels, and reaching as high as the top of the door, was a broad band of handsome paper of full toned colour and pretty modern pattern. This band was finished at the top with a narrow shelf or cornice, on which were ranged a few china plates and vases and a jug or two. Above the cornice the wall was either painted or papered of a pale grey blue, and a few Japanese-looking birds had been cut out in paper and stuck on here and there, the whole effect being that of air and space above the height of one's head.

Over the chimney-piece, which was handsome, but not remarkable, was an ingenious arrangement, a very mantel-board. The owner of the house, who himself designed and carried out all the decoration, happened to know of a country church in which what is technically termed "restoration" was going on. Restoration in this case consisted chiefly in turning out a series of fine solid oak-panelled pews in favour of the orthodox stained deal "sittings" of modern Gothic. The panelling was of course sold at a moderate rate and was, no doubt, for the most part converted into firewood, or applied to the use as *wain's cote*, or waggon sides, from which oak planking derives its usual name. One large piece was purchased and brought to London and forms the chimney-board in the room of which I speak. It is about six feet wide by seven or eight high, magnificently framed with deeply cut mouldings, in the style of the last century. A cornice has been added, partly to finish it at the top. partly to serve as a shelf. In the centre an oblong panel has been filled with looking-glass. Two or three brackets have been added at the sides, each supporting a little work of art, whether in china or ivory or bronze. The whole thing is suspended above the chimney-piece and can be taken down and hung up again in another house if necessary.

I have said nothing about painting wood-work : but in the drawing-room I have just endeavoured to describe, the door—there was but one—was in two shades of blue to harmonise with the paper and there were some gold mouldings which looked well on the blue.

I need say nothing against graining, and would not even mention it but that I heard with great surprise that in a very fine house lately remodelled and decorated in London, the owner imported painters from Paris and had his doors made to imitate walnut, mahogany, and other woods, at an expense which would have paid for the doors in the genuine material.

CHAPTER III

PICTURES.

ICTURES and prints are perhaps more connected in our minds with Art at Home than furniture. And to a certain extent our homes are more dependent on such things for decoration and for the pleasant air which a little art diffuses than on the character of the furniture. And pictures have two advantages over every other kind of art for household purposes. They are cheap and they are movable.

When I say that pictures are cheap, it must be explained that by the word picture I mean every description of drawing, printing, engraving, and photograph. But much of the kind which is hung on people's walls does not decorate them, and much, too, is a positive disfigurement. I want, therefore in this chapter to try and find a few safe rules by which a man who desires to have pictorial decorations for his . rooms may manage to do it, and to do it without loss.

Such is the problem before us. I have so far prejudged the case that I have said pictures are a cheap form of decoration. I can best illustrate my meaning by an anecdote or two.

It is well-known that Mr. Gillott of Birmingham commenced to buy pictures, not only before he was wealthy, but before he knew much about art. Yet he had a natural eye for paintings and could tell what was good from what was bad, though, perhaps, he could not have distinguished genuine from counterfeit. As soon as he could afford it he used to visit the Royal Academy and buy from a young artist. It was, not until comparatively late in life that he ventured to commission a picture. But Mr. Gillott only bought new pictures. All that were in the famous sale at Christie's were modern, or at least had been modern when they went to Mr. Gillott's gallery, having been bought from living artists. And, as I remarked in my introductory chapter, the pictures which fetched the highest prices were those for which he had given the least. He had seen merit in a work of a young artist and had bought it at a very moderate price. The next purchase was perhaps from a different artist at the same rate. And perhaps a third would come from a well-known and highly prized painter like Etty. But in the course of years, one of the younger artists would have failed to become great, a second would have succeeded, and a great man would have fallen back. Thus, one of the highest

prices was the 3,950*l.* given at the sale for Müller's
Chess Players, which cost Mr. Gillott, some 60*l.*, while
the Ettys for which he gave great sums sold for a few
hundreds apiece at most, and some of them did not
even reach " three figures." So that the Müller had
to pay for the others. Had Mr. Gillott known a little
more about art when he began to buy he might have
depended on his own judgment, and only bought
from such men as Müller, and there would have been
no drawback as in the case of his Ettys.

It was the same with Mr. Wynn Ellis, who
deserves, even more than Mr. Gillott, to be remembered in the annals of English art; for though he
did not "make people steel pens," he left the choice
of his Old Masters to our National Gallery. Of the
404 of which the collection consisted, most of which,
as I am informed, Mr. Ellis considered genuine, the
selectors have only accepted some 70. It will therefore
be understood that he was not by any means a first-
rate judge. I mention this to show that without
being a judge of the genuineness of a picture, it may
yet be possible for a man to choose what is good.
For Mr. Ellis certainly had some good pictures, and
one of his it is which has, up to the date of this
writing, the reputation of having brought the highest
price ever given for a modern picture. The reason the
so-called " Portrait of the Duchess of Devonshire
by Gainsborough " fetched more than 10,000*l.*
was simple enough. It was very pretty. No one
who saw it could help being charmed with it. As
a critic observed, it was as graceful as a Reynolds,
as pretty as a Lawrence, and as full of expression as

a Gainsborough. It was not a matter of much consequence that it bore a damaged reputation, and that
persons of authority were not wanting who said it
was not the Duchess of Devonshire and was not by
Gainsborough. I do not say the 10,000*l.* was not a
very high price, and though it may be generally
assumed that a thing is worth what it fetches, it
would be rash to prophecy that this picture will ever
bring so much again.

And it was the same, also, with a greater collector
than either Mr. Gillott or Mr. Ellis. Judgment and
taste, not money, were Mr. Sheepshanks's capital. He
was able to recognise good work when he saw it, and
though good work was not very common in the days
when he began to buy, he got what there was of it,
and he not only benefited art by bringing together
what was worth looking at, but he encouraged young
artists to greater efforts. Nothing can be more difficult
than for an artist to struggle on in spite of the sneers
of friends and relations, while, though he works never
so hard, he makes no money, perhaps, for years. He
is constantly tempted to paint " pot-boilers," and will
often sell his best pictures at prices which do not cover
the expenses he has been at in painting them. No
doubt, occasionally, a man who believes in himself and
his own work may do work which is in reality bad
and undeserving of encouragement. There are many
people willing to say that Blake is an example of this
kind, and that the French artist Corot is another.
Corot worked for years without encouragement, and
then was run up to such prices that his last years were
passed in affluence. Blake was never appreciated by

the public in his life-time; and even now it is seriously
questioned by some how far he deserves his reputation.
Both Corot and Blake, however, must have had quali-
ties in them which appealed to certain minds.   They
must have had a mission to touch certain hearts. I do
not disparage them if I say that the young collector
will do well to avoid such artists, if only because they
are uncertain.   Some men are attracted by one kind
of work, and some by another, and you may be a
good judge of what you like and a poor judge of
what you do not like.   But, on the whole, eccen-
tric work is doubtful, and a picture which requires
the help of a showman to point out its meaning and
its beauty, is but half a picture.   Mr. Sheepshanks,
however, had powers of discrimination in art and
needed no one to tell him that the young Edwin
Landseer was working hard and could touch the
feelings of a large and enlarging audience.   It is said
that the first picture Mr. Sheepshanks ever bought
was Landseer's *Twa Dogs* and that he gave the young
artist 30*l.* for it.   How much is it worth now ?   About
a hundred times thirty.

If, therefore, your knowledge and taste are such
that you can be sure of recognising good work, and if
you have a little money to lay out, you cannot do a
more judicious thing than to buy from young artists.
You do a kindness to them, and you, so to speak, back
your own opinion.

Next to buying from young artists, you may buy
"old masters."   There is, perhaps, no branch of trade,
not even excepting horse-dealing, in which there is
more deceit and chicanery than in picture-dealing.

The commercial axiom that supply always equals demand is as true in the old picture market as in any other. If a master comes to the front, is written up by Mr. Ruskin, or is brought into fashion for any other reason, his works suddenly find their way into the market from all sorts of unexpected places. Who had ever heard, out of art circles, of Piero della Francesca, when Mr. Barker's pictures caused so much controversy a few years ago? Immediately afterwards Pieros were quite common. Every dealer's shop contained one, all were equally genuine, and dozens, perhaps hundreds, of collectors were taken in. Rembrandts are manufactured by the thousand. Had the artist been a Briareus he could not have painted even the pictures which are said to be authentic. If you go in for old masters, therefore, you lay yourself out for a prey to the designing, and unless you are a really excellent judge of art you will be taken in over and over again. I could fill this whole volume with stories of people who have been thus deceived. One old lady, who bought a *Crucifixion* for fifty guineas and asked a few good judges to see it, and was never on good terms with them afterwards ; one young gentleman who squandered his patrimony, meaning when he came to his last penny to sell the Coreggios and Claudes his father had paid so high for, and who was mortified to find they were only worth as many shillings as they had cost pounds; the learned literary man who was deceived by a contemporary portrait of Shakespeare ; these and many other cases occur to me ; and the first advice I should give anyone who proposed to embark in old masters would be, "Don't."

But old pictures are dangerous for another reason besides that just indicated. They are not only liable to forgery and imitation, but they are very liable to fluctuations of taste. Some of us remember well when Mr. Ruskin began to write up Turner and write down Claude. People who had Claudes were in despair. Pictures bought for thousands sold for hundreds, and Turner himself was induced to commit the incredible folly of leaving certain paintings to be hung in the National Gallery beside the masterpieces of Claude. Turners are still very valuable, and those which contain good work will always be very valuable, but Turner's poor work is worth very little, and Claudes are probably as valuable now as they ever were. Meanwhile people who wanted to sell their Claudes must have lost heavily. Another master who has fluctuated very much is Murillo. Good Murillos have been sold very cheap of late years. No doubt they may recover, but it would be hazardous to buy them on speculation.

But, as I shall have occasion to point out by and by, there is one thing which will always command a price, namely, honest hard work. The highly finished pictures of the great Dutch school are liable to less fluctuation than any other works of art. They steadily and quietly increase in estimation. Mr. Ruskin cannot write them down if he would. And the reason is easily found. They contain good, downright, hard work ; they are not scamped ; there is no "execution" for execution's sake in them, as there is in Murillo ; and, for the most part, their subjects, though homely, are of a kind which will always command popularity even with those who know little or nothing about art.

If you must have old pictures, it will not be difficult to point out a few rules for your guidance. Do not expect to find good old pictures for a small price. The sources from which such works come are thoroughly well examined. A cheap old master can hardly be a good one, so do not think a picture good merely because it is old. Not only are some genuine old pictures worthless, but some genuine pictures by great painters are equally without value. A man may pick up a Morland, for instance, at a very low price, yet there are few of the early English school, as it is called, which command a better price than his good works. The young amateur often hears a good name attached to a picture, and has every reason to believe it is painted by the artist to whom it is attributed, yet finds that it is to be had at a low price and so thinks it must be cheap. And I have known several men who have filled their rooms with Cromes, and Turners, and Constables, and Ettys, all of them "picked up for a song." Such questionable bargains are to be had in plenty. But they are only worth what they will fetch, namely, the "song" aforesaid, and they are not pretty or pleasant to look at or else they would have commanded better prices. It is not uncommon to see the walls of a room hung with inferior Turners and Constables, and other little works of great artists. The names on the frames have a very fine appearance. They may even be said in some cases to be rather ornamental; but the pictures to which they are annexed are valueless in the market and are not pleasant to the eye.

Old pictures that have been restored are also a bad investment. Of such pictures there are two kinds at least. First those which are overlaid with inferior work; and second, those which never were good. The principles of "restoration" are rather complicated. The dealer who wants a purchaser to think a picture genuine works in one way. The dealer who wants a purchaser to think he is about to buy a good picture but overlaid with inferior painting works in a different way, though the result is the same. The purchaser is taken in. He may say, "Here is a good painting by a first-rate hand; injured, perhaps, and mended; covered with rough paint, and varnished a great deal too much." The amateur is perhaps anxious to perform the necessary processes of restoration for himself, and he buys the Van Eyck or the Crome of Norwich and sets to work. After he has taken off the varnish he finds there is very little left; and by the time the panel or canvas is completely cleaned the chances are he has nothing at all but the canvas left. But in spite of one or two cases to the contrary which I shall mention, it may be taken for granted, that the best face of which the picture is capable is put forward, and that the restoration, if it is bad, is bad for a purpose, and if it is good is the best that can be made.

There are two remarkable instances of good pictures having been discovered under bad ones. The famous Correggio, *Egeria* or *Mary Magdalene*, which was painted over with a landscape, in order, no doubt, to escape the vigilance of customhouse officers, or the

E 2

cupidity of French soldiers, was discovered by a cleaner, and is now one of the gems of Lord Dudley's gallery. Another example was that of the unfinished picture by Michael Angelo of the Entombment, now in the National Gallery, which had a picture of some importance on the surface. In this case, the unfinished sketch of the great master was probably not thought to be worth preserving. But these two examples, and a very few, if any more, are really responsible for great destructions and for wonderful probing of varnishes, and for many a purchase of bad pictures. The amateur may be pretty certain that the dealer knows his own business best, and that a bargain is very seldom to be had.

Old Masters, then, which profess to be genuine, can only be offered cheap when their authenticity is doubtful and when they are disagreeable in subject.

But in choosing them, as well as in choosing all works of art, the young collector cannot go wrong if he prefer what is pretty and good for its own sake Where you have a pleasant subject like the *Duchess of Devonshire*, the history of the picture is of secondary importance. When Mr. Wynn Ellis gave 63*l*. for it because he liked it, he did a much wiser thing than when he paid vastly higher prices for pictures with great names and magnificent pedigrees, which Mr. Burton has not cared to hang.

I cannot too strongly impress it, that though a good name is a good thing for a picture to have, it is a far better thing for the picture itself to be good. One of the best pictures in the National Gallery has no artist's name to it, the beautiful *Knight adoring the Holy Family*, which is believed to be of the Venetian School. On the other hand, some of the worst pictures have good pedigrees, as Titian's and Leonardo da Vinci's, and, no doubt, cost their late proprietors large sums. A picture is not an autograph. Because a great man's hand has been over it, and because, perhaps, it bears his signature, it is not necessarily valuable. Look, for example, at many of the hideous daubs which bear Rembrandt's hand writing, and, almost without doubt, came from his studio and were really signed by him. They are unpleasant to look at, whether they are really by Rembrandt or only by Van Eckhout, his pupil, but for a time they deluded buyers, and we have one of the largest and worst in our National Gallery. With them compare the modest pictures by P. de Hooghe. A few years ago this great painter's name was absolutely unknown to the general public, and his works were attributed to other artists. Yet they are now among the most expensive pictures you can buy, and they well deserve their popularity, for they are full of the best and most conscientious work.

The principles on which to choose modern pictures are not very different from those which apply to old masters. When a man buys to decorate his walls, and not to sell again, it need not very much signify what names are attached to his pictures. There are pictures which bear Mr. Cope's name, and also Mr. O'Neil's, which would be an ornament to any collection, and I cannot believe that if they were to be offered at Christie's they would fetch poor prices, even though the artists in question have not been at the pains.

to sustain their early reputation. Young artists must
be chosen entirely on their merits, and when a new
painter promises well and turns out badly, the buyer
of his early works loses by him ; that is, he loses if
he thinks to get a profit.

The safeguard against loss of this kind, however, is
very simple. Do not confine yourself to the work of
one artist ; and, unless your taste runs very decidedly
in one direction, do not confine yourself to a single
school. It is said that the buyers of works by Mr.
Burne Jones and Mr. Rossetti and other pictures of
the so-called " pre-Raphaelite" class cannot take any
pleasure in ordinary painting. I do not wonder at it ;
but if they buy for their own pleasure only, it does not
matter. If, however, they have an idea that some
day their collections may be sold with other assets
of their personal estate, they must leaven their
"advanced" works with a few of the kind people
usually prefer.

And it may be necessary to give intending patrons
of art another caution. Do not encourage bad painting. We often see a boy taken up by a country
circle, and puffed and praised till he thinks himself a
prodigy—all because he may have a happy trick of
hitting a likeness, or may have a little more power
than the ordinary sketching amateur. Local magnates
buy his works, and provincial mayors have their portraits done, and he goes up to London, or some other
centre, and enters a school. Sometimes he succeeds.
It was thus that John Philip came to London. But
in a great majority of cases such patrons know
nothing about art, and think it a marvellous thing that

anyone can draw a likeness or a landscape without special training, although every ploughboy who can whistle a tune without musical training is not of necessity a Mozart or a Purcell in disguise. In some foreign countries, as, for instance in Japan or Italy, everybody draws, just as here everybody whistles, but a talent for painting pictures is a long way beyond sketching, just as a talent for composing oratorios is a long way beyond singing popular melodies.

There are young gentlemen, in London especially, who practise art with an idea that it is not only the pleasure but the duty of patrons to buy from them, and that a man has no right to have any views on the merits of a picture but those taught him by the artist. These loquacious artists talk of the poetry of æsthetics till the listener wishes he could dose them with anæsthetics, and in many cases they persuade men who do not know much about art that their works are superb. The purchaser of such pictures is astonished when he gets one of these wonderful productions home to find it looks ill beside his other pictures, and that, for the life of him he is unable to explain its meaning to his wife or his visitor, though the artist had such a glowing story to tell. It may be assumed as an axiom that, as I said before, a picture which does not tell its own story is but half a picture, and that these young gentlemen who can talk so much are not likely ever to have time to spare to learn painting. You are doing an injury to good art and hard-working artists when you encourage such people in idleness, for, after all, it is idleness; and it is but a false kind of good nature which urges you to buy from them.

A little while ago an artist came to a lady well known both for her liberal charities and also for her interest in spiritualism. The gentleman told her that he had received in a trance the design of a picture, and that he was very anxious to paint it, but, though he described to her very fully the ideas he had, he delayed or hesitated to put them on canvas. The lady, after she had seen him several times, took so much interest in the work, or was so much influenced by the glowing imagery and flowing eloquence of the spiritualist painter, that she commissioned him to paint the scene. He still hesitated. She suspected that he wanted money for models and other such like purposes, and generously offered him a cheque in part payment for the unpainted picture. The fact was he hesitated because he knew that to paint such a picture as he had described was wholly beyond his powers. I do not say that he meant dishonestly. I only know, from his previous work, that he was absolutely incapable of painting anything well, and that his only endurable pictures were some fairly accurate likenesses, in which all the details of drapery and background were ill drawn and worse coloured. As to painting the gates of heaven, and the spirit of the deceased husband of the lady, as he had appeared to the artist, coming to welcome his wife to the realms of bliss, the subject was as much beyond his utmost powers as if he had undertaken to pay the National Debt or swim to New York.

However, he set to work. I believe he conscientiously thought he had seen the vision : and also, that he should be able to make a picture of it, expecting, perhaps, some help from another world. Be this as it may, the picture went on, and the lady was charmed as the design became more apparent. She again gave him money, until the whole sum promised had been spent. At last the artist, I suppose, found he could do no more; he took the picture home. The poor woman was sadly disappointed. It did not answer her expectations. She knew nothing about art, but fancied she knew a good deal, and the picture did not satisfy either her taste or her expectations. The artist, however, though he could not paint, could talk, and before the interview was over had persuaded his patron not only "that there was a great deal in the picture," but also that as a painting it would have been a great deal better if the means at his disposal had been larger. The lady hesitated : she would consult her friends. They condemned the picture with ridicule. Something must be done with it. She could not bring herself to burn it, for it had cost her much money. So the artist was recalled and set to work again with a "refresher." The process may be going on still, *da capo*, for aught I can tell to the contrary, and the artist has probably a small income out of his picture, but if not it must be owing to the failure of his eloquence.

You may be quite certain that a young man who is willing to work and really able to learn painting, will have but a moderate difficulty in getting into the School of the Royal Academy, in which, after all, the majority of the best English artists of all kinds are educated. When an artist beginning life has not per-severance enough to make the very slight exertion necessary to pass the entrance examination, it must be a very sanguine patron that will spend any large sum on his pictures. There are cases, no doubt, where a man of taste and knowledge will venture to back his own opinion. But such cases hardly come within the scope of the present treatise.

Instead of pictures, either ancient or modern, prints may be chosen for decoration. Strange as it may seem, more taste and knowledge are required in the choice of prints than in the choice of paintings. Few of the rules for picture-buying apply to print-buying. For instance, it is much safer and wiser to buy old masters of engraving than new. Restoration of prints is on a very different footing from restoration of pictures. A torn plate may be mended. A margin may be put on a close clipped print, but no one can make a bad impression into a good one, or produce an imitation of Rembrandt or Dürer at such a cost as to make it worth the trouble. Photography has enabled some foreign cheats to produce prints with which to deceive tourists, but no one acquainted with the originals could have been deceived for a moment. If the copy of a print is as good as the original it is as valuable. There was some talk in art circles a few years ago about an unsigned print, for which a collector had given a long price. Wise people said the print had been sold as a Marc Antonio, and as being unique, but that it was not a Marc Antonio, and that another impression existed. But the fact is neither of these questions affected the beauty of the print. Whether engraved by Marc or by one of his pupils, it was well engraved. Whether absolutely unique or not, no other impression had ever occurred for sale. In either case, and at all events, it was a beautiful work and therefore of value.

Prints may be roughly divided into two great classes. Those in which the engraver has interpreted his own design, and those in which he has copied from a picture by some one else.

The French call original engravers *peintres graveurs*. The works of Dürer and Rembrandt, of Meryon and Mr. Seymour Haden, are all of this kind.

Marc Antonio, though he made some engravings of his own designs, chiefly copied Raffaelle or Titian ; and in our own day Thomas Landseer has both produced etchings of his own and has also engraved his more famous brother's pictures.

The great majority of modern engravers have only copied from pictures. Such were Smith and others, who made mezzotints from Reynolds, and whose works sometimes fetch very high prices. We have frequently seen a single print by Smith after Reynolds bring more than Reynolds obtained for the original picture.

On the whole, for decorative purposes, modern prints are the best where there is plenty of wall space, and ancient, being smaller, where there is little. As prints do not suffer by being exposed to the light, but are injured by being rubbed together in portfolios, it seems strange that we do not more often see good engravings hung on the walls. A *Melencholia* by Dürer, or a *Burgomaster Six* by Rembrandt, is eminently decorative. It gives a room an air which some of the best modern pictures would fail to impart.

Good Landseer prints, too, are very ornamental in
frames, but terribly unwieldy and liable to tearing in
a portfolio.

Old prints by a *peintre graveur* are, on the whole,
the best for the judicious collector. He can choose a
master, say one of Dürer's pupils, and buy quietly good
impressions, here and there, hanging them in frames
where he can see them, and comparing impressions
until he has a good collection. He will find that
great pleasure is to be derived from the pursuit, that
it increases incidentally his knowledge of other kinds
of art, and that, unless he is very extravagant, he
is making a perfectly safe investment of his money.

Many years ago Dibdin praised the works of one
of these "little masters," as they are called, namely,
Hans Sebald Beham, and had two *facsimiles* made
from his engravings. But they never seem to have
come much into fashion. I cannot imagine any old
master whose works are better suited for decorative
purposes in a small town house. They are all very
small, some of the best being only two inches long by
one high, but they are very pretty in sets in a frame,
and are, for the most part, in the highest style of the
high German art of the time.

I subjoin a reversed copy from Beham's version of
the *Melencholia*, partly because it is another render-
ing of Dürer's famous subject, and partly because
it seems to be less known than it should be.

All the older engravings have greatly increased in
value of late years, and as they are no longer to be
had in good condition at prices which bring them into
ordinary competition with modern works, I will not.

delay over them, except just to offer a few rules to the collector.

You may safely give a high price for a unique impression, or for any impression in an early state. Proofs of old prints are not always recognised. If

you have knowledge of the subject, you may feel very secure in this respect.

Secondly, it is better to have a few good impressions than a complete set of a master in an inferior condition. In order to form a thorough acquaintance with the work of an artist, it is sometimes necessary to have poor impressions to compare with good. But this is a point on which much might be written, and it does not exactly enter into our subject, being rather a matter for discussion in a treatise on prints.

It is better to have a common print which is interesting in subject than a much superior one which is unpleasant or ugly. It is necessary to include this among our cautions, because it often happens that the old masters differed from us moderns in their ideas of what is good taste, and though some of Dürer's prettiest prints are the most common, they always fetch their price, and are eagerly sought after. I allude especially to such engravings as his *Knight of Death*, his *Melencholia*, and his four beautiful little *Madonnas* with the crescent. You may be deceived into buying a print because it is cheap, but you will generally find, if it is a good impression, that on account of the subject it is not fit to be hung up, and that you have therefore given its full value. As success in collecting prints greatly depends on having a good eye for states and impressions, the wise collector will constantly compare what he possesses with the best examples in public museums.

The buying of modern prints is a very different thing. I have already in my introductory chapter told the story of a man who was induced to buy "proofs" at great cost without knowing enough about the subject His fate was a common one. The word "proof" has been corrupted from its ancient usage. It originally meant a trial impression taken of a plate to see how it approached completion. Such impressions were supposed, partly because of their rarity, and partly because of their being early and unworn, to be more valuable than prints from the completed plate. After a time " proofs " were held to include impressions taken after the engraver had done with his work and before the caligrapher had engraved the title. Later impressions taken with " open letters," that is while the letters of the title were still in outline, were added to the lengthening list. But the crowning absurdity was reserved for the deception of buyers in our own day. Prints are now " published " by publishers, just like books, and they advertise the prices without much reference to the state of the plate. The number of proofs is in most cases, and especially where the publisher is unscrupulous, only limited by the number of subscribers, and I have heard, on good or bad authority, that of one modern popular print there were six thousand " proofs " taken.

Line engraving is now almost extinct, and more rapid work, either mezzotint or a combination of mezzotint and line is in fashion with engravers. But the whole condition of engraving was altered when the process of " steeling " a plate was invented, and good impressions may still be had after many thousands have been taken off. After a large number of so-called proofs have been printed the plate is often retouched by the engraver, so that it sometimes happens that a " proof " is not so good as an ordinary impression.

In works on copper, however, there is much more variety. It may safely be said that of a delicate etching no two impressions are alike. The collector is very safe if he has selected judiciously, but it

seems to me that there is a great want of better
art in such things. The most ardent admirer of
modern etching has little opportunity of buying
anything except landscapes, and of them very few
that are of an interesting type. When modern etchers
go back to figure subjects such as Rembrandt studied,
and to chiaroscuro like his, they will be well worthy
of attention. But to the general taste Mr. Whistler's
ragged style of rapid execution is absolutely without
meaning, and Mr. Legros' figures are too unpleasing,
too rigid, too slight, to be attractive except in the
eyes of those who are educated in etching.

For, it must be remembered, in buying prints to
hang on our walls, that we do not live alone in our
houses, but that what we hang is for the entertainment
of our guests and for the instruction of our children,
and only for our own enjoyment in a secondary degree.
The object of this book, as I have already more than
once pointed out, is to help a man who wishes to bring
art home. Why the modern efforts of the "aqua-
fortist" should be so greatly concerned with landscape, I cannot tell, except it be that professional
artists who are in the habit of drawing the figure are
too busy to engrave, and that the copper-plates are
left chiefly to amateurs to whom landscape is more
possible than figure. Such amateurs are and were
Mr. Haden, Mr. Hamerton, the famous Meryon, who
was, I believe, a lieutenant in the French navy, and
many others who have become known in this branch
of art. The few professional artists who have taken
to it are chiefly of what may be called the landscape
persuasion. But it is much to be hoped that before

long the list of *peintres graveurs* may contain a
larger number of young names, and that even the
dry point and the admirable line of Dürer and Marc
Antonio and the Behams may revisit the earth.

Turner's *Liber Studiorum* stands at the head
of all modern copper-plate work. To know these
prints thoroughly, to be able at sight to distinguish
the states and to tell bad from good, is a science in
itself. Of late years they have been very much
sought after, and good impressions have become
exceedingly scarce. But now and then fair examples
of odd prints are to be had, and they are, on the
whole, very decorative, especially if mounted on a
grey or blue paper.

Two or three minor kinds of art may be said to
come under the denomination of "pictures," such
as woodcuts or photographs. They may be briefly
dismissed. Woodcuts, at least modern ones, are seldom
effective when hung on a wall. For such a purpose
are almost always unsuited. It seems to be the great
object of modern engravers to make the cut as like
a steel engraving as possible, and if you frame one
of the great pictures with which the illustrated papers
"present" the public now and then, you will be disappointed at its appearance on the wall. It looks
only like a worn-out print, or like a very hard mezzotint at best. A few of the older wood artists made
attempts at producing good decorative pictures for
a wall. There are some very fine shaded and tinted
copies of Tintoretto which have a large handsome
effect, and the style might be revived with advantage.
The slightly shaded works of Dürer on wood, though

they are generally too quaint to be very pleasing, may yet be found to look well in frames. But I do not think I know any modern wood engravings of a large size which are suitable for hanging as decorations. The moment wood-engravers began to attempt what was impossible, in cross-hatching, for example, they lost the life which was the essence of their art.

Whether photographs can be considered decorative is a matter of some controversy from this point of view. I should be sorry to condemn them. On the contrary, I think good photographs of scenery, of buildings, and of archæological remains generally, are both interesting and beautiful. They do not look well on the same wall with water-colours, and the man who buys many should remember that they will probably fade before long, and that the same money spent on one picture might do something for the encouragement and improvement of real art. But people who travel much find no record of places they have seen so faithful as photography, and it is pleasant to lean back in one's chair and be transported to distant countries at a glance.

Photography is of little use for portraiture. I mean that large pictures of landscapes in photography are much more common and more pleasing than large likenesses. The vulgar staring portraits produced by many photographers do not bear enlargement, but Mrs. Cameron and others have shown us that in this respect much is possible, and the day may come when people will have their "ancestors" well and pleasantly photographed.

I have purposely said little about portraits as pictures. People who have family pictures do not take them down because they are ill done. The whole subject of portraiture, so far as it enters into the scope of this little book, is to be considered less as art than as something to be calculated upon and allowed for. A man can no more help his family portraits being hideous or ill painted than he can help being born the heir of an estate in one county rather than in another. He must endeavour, if the bulk of his portraits are of a particular period, as so often occurs owing to some passage in the family history, such as an access of wealth or position, to assimilate the furniture and surroundings to the costume of his ancestors. I have known an insolent young gentleman who sent his family portraits to the bedrooms because they did not agree with his new Gothic furniture; but I think such a man did not deserve to be blest with ancestors of which he had no other reason to be ashamed.

In a different case a gentleman had about twenty little crayon drawings of the family of his grandfather early in the last century, and he arranged them round the walls of a room alternately with ornamental panels containing shields of arms, with the happiest effect.

This question of arrangement is one of the most important with which art at home is concerned. It is often said that only water-colours should hang in the drawing-room, and portraits in the dining-room. But all such hard and fast rules are absurd. The true rule is to put the pictures where they look best.

One of the accompanying woodcuts shows a room

in which oil-pictures and water-colours have been mixed. It is a drawing-room, and has already been mentioned (p. 39). On the wall to the left of the cut hangs a row of water-colours. As the owner considers them all worth looking at, and as he takes much pleasure in looking at them himself and in showing them to his friends, he has hung them in a straight line opposite the eye. Strange to say the effect is not at all formal, and for a simple reason. The pictures are of various sizes and shapes, and only the bottom of each frame ranges with the bottom of the next. The tops are at all levels. The same effect might have been attained by having the tops all level, and the bottoms irregular. The row consists wholly of water-colours; but oil pictures, especially portraits, might very well be disposed on the walls above.

For the most part, a dark red ground is the best for pictures, especially old ones in oil, but the frames must be adapted to prevent the wall paper from interfering with the pictures. To isolate a painting from its surroundings is, indeed, the final cause of frames, and to make the frame more ornamental than the picture, seems to me little less than a crime.

Hanging is a fine art in itself. A well-arranged gallery is as rare as a well-painted picture, and the rules most often given are of little use. Even experienced people are often puzzled how to show their possessions to the best advantage. What suits one picture does not suit another, and it is impossible to say before hand what will look best. For my own part, I think the great object of having pictures is that they may be looked at, and at the risk of ruining the symmetry of my room I am inclined to hang them where I can see them with the most ease. Mr. Wynn Ellis had movable shutters to suit different lights and hung his pictures on them. But most owners of pictures will prefer to consider them as ornaments of the house, and will place them where both the pictures are at the greatest advantage and the room itself is most ornamented by the pictures. To hit this mean is not easy, but since no two pictures and no two rooms are exactly alike it must be left to the taste and pleasure of the owner to dispose his pictures in his rooms as they seem to him to look best.

I cannot conclude this chapter without some reference to art in the nursery. Putting aside toys and books for the present, there is still much scope for pictures on the walls. Children study such things much more than some people suppose. They remember them long afterwards, and many a child looks back to the picture which hung over his bed years and years after other and better pictures might have been expected to drive it out of his head. The importance of supplying children with examples of good art cannot be insisted on too much. Their taste may be warped unconsciously by some piece of poor design, or some gaudy inharmonious colouring. When a child is working at music we do not let the piano get out of tune, lest the little performer's ear should be spoiled. But we think much more of the subject of the nursery pictures than of their merit as designs, and never remember that the children may have in after life to complain of an inability to judge of colour, or a deficient eye for form owing to our neglect.

It is not easy, I confess, to obtain good pictures for the nursery wall.   On the whole rather than hang up some of the poverty-stricken scriptural subjects which are to be had, I should be inclined to use the worn-out engravings of good pictures which may be bought so cheap, and which have no prominent fault, though they are pale and weak.   A child's taste may be greatly influenced by the habitual contemplation of a print after Raffaelle, or Rembrandt.   I am glad to hear that an effort is being made by one of the educational societies to take up the questions here suggested, and to enable us to decorate the walls of the nursery and schoolroom with prints whose teaching will not have to be unlearned if possible in after life.

CHAPTER IV.

BOOKS AND CHINA.

VERY reader may not agree with me if I say that pictures ornament a house more than anything else, but that next to pictures I am inclined to place books. Most people would perhaps give the precedence to china. But if china is really valuable it is too fragile to be used for decorative purposes, and if it is left out of the cabinet it may be broken. An exception must be made in favour of the very beautiful earthenware of Flanders and Germany, but almost all other kinds of pottery are very fragile. Books on the other hand, are very indestructible, and I cannot help thinking a well-filled bookcase one of the best ornaments of any sitting-room.

Ornamental books may be roughly divided into

three classes, manuscripts, books of prints, and books whose binding is their chief feature. A word should also be said about nursery literature since it is often from " toy books " that young people derive their first ideas on art.

Manuscripts which contain illuminations have an altogether exceptional character. If we look at them as pictures painted before the modern schools of oil-painting were instituted we shall not be far wrong. A book of " Hours " will sometimes contain a series of designs by a great but anonymous artist who flourished perhaps a century before Raffaelle. For such a "pocket gallery " we may have to pay less than for a single picture by an artist of the same period. This is sometimes very strange, and must be chiefly owing to the want of intelligent books on the greatest of the art of the middle ages. There is no classification into styles and schools, no attempt to identify various works of the same artist. I can promise the industrious amateur who wants employment for his leisure hours, not only a great deal of pleasure, but also the warm thanks of all connoisseurs if he will take the books in a public collection and classify them with some reference to period, school of art, country, and individual artist.

To many people it will be new to hear that we had a school of art in England in the twelfth and thirteenth centuries such as we have never had since, and that there were painters and sculptors among our ancestors in the reign of Henry III. whose works excel anything that has been produced in our island in the nineteenth century.

The initial letters of the chapters of this book are taken from Bibles of that period written in England, because such Bibles are among the most common examples of this style of art, while they best illustrate my meaning, owing to the identity of the subjects in several. Jonah in the act of falling into the jaws of the whale, or else just rising from them again, is a favourite subject and is sometimes treated with exceeding quaintness. The crossbar letter E, with which in the Latin the Book of Jonah commences, was made use of to give the picture a kind of upper story.

In buying manuscripts the great difficulty consists in knowing whether they are perfect or not. It would be impossible to give rules for the purpose of assisting a buyer in the space at my disposal, but I may venture a caution as to two of the most common of such books. In Missals always look for a painting of the crucifixion. If this is wanting the book is almost certainly imperfect. In books of " Hours," you may be equally particular in seeking a calendar. Without a calendar the book would have been practically useless, and I cannot believe any book of " Hours " is perfect without some sort of calendar.

Of manuscripts, too, it may safely be said that some of the most gaudy are the least valuable, and that the judicious buyer will prefer that which has an especially quaint treatment of a subject, or any sign of being the work of an original and untrammelled mind.

Modern illustrated books may be very briefly dismissed. The best have woodcuts, the worst have chromo-lithographs ; but it may be worth while to

point out that different copies of an illustrated book
have very different impressions of the pictures ; an'i
that a late edition of one of Bewick's books, for
example, is a very inferior work to an early edition.

There has been a kind of run on early woodcuts of
late years, and we are at length, after centuries of
neglect, beginning to recognize the beauty of the early
French school—that of Paris, from which issued so
many devotional books in the fifteenth century, and
the early part of the sixteenth, as well as of the later
school,—and that of Lyons, from which issued so many
exquisitely illustrated Bibles, Testaments, Dances of
Death, Emblems, and other books, all now become
exceedingly valuable, though once, not many years
ago, to be had very cheap. If we could tell what will
be the next fashion we might commence collecting
now, and make a fortune when the tide turns. The
French are busy at present with books illustrated
with copper-plate vignettes, and chiefly belonging to
the period before the Revolution. But we have little
art to show for that period in England, and must come
down to the times of Stothard and Westall for something original and good of native growth.

The book collector may, however, form a collection
of many kinds of books different from any already the
fashion. If he buy with knowledge he can hardly
lose by it, but the kind of knowledge required is rathei
literary than artistic, and does not exactly belong to
our subject. So I will pass on at once, only pausing
to encourage the book collector with an anecdote
relating to circumstances which lately occurred. A
gentleman happened to stroll into a saleroom during

a sale of books, and seeing an unbound book full of engravings, and described as a Sarum Service-book, he bid 5*l.* for it, imagining it to be worth much more. It was knocked down to him, however, and for months he amused his leisure with that book. First he went to the British Museum and soon ascertained that no example of the same edition was in the library there. Then he had it handsomely bound, and taking it to Oxford and other places compared it with various specimens, sometimes finding a fragment of the same edition bound into another book, and once a very imperfect copy wanting the large cuts. At last he grew tired of his toy, and having written a full account of its beauties and peculiarities he put it up at an auction and received 36*l.* for it. This example speaks for itself.

The nursery literature of the present day is one of the wonderful things of our wonderful age. Children are indeed provided for in this respect better than their parents were when they grew up. Many a child has a library that would have sufficed a hundred years ago for a country town.

Mr. Marks led the way in seeing the difficulty of making good "toy books." His nursery rhymes marked an epoch in pictorial literature. Since then Mr. Crane and others have taken up the tale, and the parent who desires to bring up a child as if harmony of colour was to be compared in importance with har· mony of sound, may easily provide that the infantine eye shall only be used to what is good.

Picture books have all the same drawback as pieces of household decoration, but bindings are sometimes

very pretty.   For the most part however our modern
bindings are hideous and one longs to go back to the
time when every book was bound in calf or sheep
at the least, if it was bound at all.

Binders follow many very objectionable practices
in binding books.   It is quite impossible to persuade
the ordinary binder, for instance, that there is any
beauty in wide margins, nay in any margin.   He
ruthlessly cuts off all such superfluities.   According
to his view the printed portion only should be left
of the page, and where he is in doubt as to whether
he has left enough margin he settles the question
by cutting a line or two of the printing at the top
and bottom.   How many valuable books have been
rendered valueless by the binder, no one can ever
know.

His enmity against margins is only equalled by his
abhorrence of fly leaves, an abhorrence extending
even to such useless things as title pages.   He argues
perhaps that the world did very well without title
pages before printing was invented, and even for
twenty or thirty years later, so that though he habitually preserves the title, more especially if told to do
so, he thinks it a vanity.   As to the half title no
persuasion can save it, and he looks on people who
preserve the covers of books issued in covers, as
simply idiotic.   Lately I had some volumes of a scarce
though modern German book on Hymnology bound.
I had bought it in numbers and gave directions that
the green paper covers should be included in the
binding.   When the book came home I found the
binder had spared the front cover, but had taken off

the other though both front and back leaves had contained notices of the greatest importance.

A still more melancholy example of the hopelessness of trying to resist fate's shears in those of the binder came before me recently. A gentleman who collected Bibles was greatly elated one day at finding a copy of one of the black-letter quartos with, as he expressed it, "the rare sheet A before the title." Bibliographers are inscrutable in all their ways, and attach great importance to such external features So he bought the book, though it was a poor copy wanting a leaf or two, and of a common edition. True, the " rare leaf A " was in all probability unique, and the happy owner broke up another copy to make this one perfect, and took his treasure to a binder, charging him to spare no expense in covering it suitably. The result is too dreadful for words, and I cannot dwell on it. But the unfortunate bibliographer had gone to great expense, and had in return a very worthless book. One wonders whether binders keep albums of rare fly leaves and title-pages.

Another, and very similar case is famous. A lady who had a nephew, wished as his birthday approached to give him a present. She knew that he greatly admired an old book in her library. It was the "First Folio" of Shakespeare, a very large copy in the original binding. She would give him this book, and thinking it looked shabby she sent it to her binder, who took off the rubbed old calf, and put the book into a neat half-binding of green roan, at the same time cutting the edges close to the text and gilding them. The lady's nephew found it difficult to express his thanks in suitable terms, for his chief, if not his only, admiration for the book consisted in its being one of the "tallest" copies in existence.

This story has, I believe, been often in print before. But not long ago I knew an almost precisely similar case in which, however, it was only a Bewick which was mutilated by being clipped close, title taken off as soiled, and the title of the second volume prefixed to the first.

There is in fact a certain excitement in sending a precious book to be bound, and the most singular thing, one of the most singular things, indeed, in the history of human nature, is the constant persistence of binders in the same habits which, for hundreds of years have caused them to be universally reprobated by all right-thinking book collectors. Roger Payne used to boast that he bound books so strongly, that they might be laid down in a pavement, and the suffering tribe of bibliographers retorted that his books were only fit for that position. But Payne did not cut a book if he could help it, and some of his modern disciples in "bibliopegistry" are quite as careful. It is only the ignorant second-rate book-binder who does the damage, but it must be allowed that whether owing to the large number of such binders, or to their amazing energy, the harm they do is enough for themselves, and for their more careful congeners too.

Bindings pleasing to the eye need not be expensive. If you fix on a pattern, you will find the cost greatly diminished by sending a dozen volumes together to the binder. Some variety of "Roxburgh" half-binding looks well, both on the shelf and on the table. As to patterns for whole bindings, we have plenty of examples, and need never be at a loss for a good one. In the woodcut I have shown two ancient books in my own collection. The smaller one may

possibly date from the fourteenth century : its two sides are not stamped with the same pattern, although they match very well, two varieties of the fret being employed. The result is very pleasing, and I can vouch for its being suitable for a modern book, as I have tried it. The principles of decoration at present in use only present two varieties, but here we have a third. We have books with one side plain and one side ornamented, or else we have both sides bearing the impression of the same pattern. But this example shows what a good effect may be produced by having the sides both ornamented but with different patterns, designed to harmonize with each other but not to match exactly.

The larger volume is equally picturesque, but not so useful for imitation. It is stamped all over with little heraldic dragons, in rows, divided by mottoes in English, and is interesting as an example of English work of the fifteenth century.

Another style of the binding would be suitable, pretty and convenient for prayer-books and hymn-books. It is such a binding as we see in the hands of Van Eyck's *Madonna* at Ghent. Service-books, which had to be carried to church, and which were constantly opened and thumbed at the same place were bound with a kind of hanging curtain or veil which both served to attach the book to its owner's belt, and also to turn up and put under the fingers during the time the book was in use. There are very few examples remaining of such a binding, but modern binders have copied some specimens from pictures.

Of later bindings much has been said and written : many fine collections have been made, but, so far, very little done as to classification and identification. The greatest French binder was probably Derome, the greatest English was Roger Payne, but bindings are chiefly distinguished by the names of the binders' patrons ; Grolier, with his motto on every book, "Grolierii et amicorum," and Thuanus, otherwise known as De Thou. There is also a very fine old English style, much sought after, and harmonizing very well with "Queen Anne" furniture and decorations.

I have perhaps spent more time on books and bindings than they deserve, considered as specimens of art at home. I have still to speak of china, of ivories, and of many other things most commonly met with in our houses.

For decorative purposes, "Oriental," that is Chinese and Japanese china, only, is worth much. Some Sèvres, and a good deal of what the modern English makers have produced of late years, is also to be admired, but chiefly in so far as it approaches the " Oriental." As to the porcelain, for which, under the names of Chelsea, Bow, and Bristol, such fabulous prices are often given, I have little or nothing to say. They are ugly, inharmonious, sometimes dingy, sometimes gaudy, and only valuable as very fragile curiosities. I cannot remember ever to have seen a beautiful example of any of these much-prized potteries. Of Worcester and Derby, on the other hand, some very beautiful specimens occasionally occur, close imitations of the Oriental patterns. It is some times quite absurd to see a plate or a bowl of Oriental ware put up and sold for a few shillings, while a similar piece, imitated from it and not nearly so good, but bearing a Worcester mark, fetches as many pounds.

The mark, indeed, generally determines the value of the china. So far we have only deciphered and identified a few of the Chinese and Japanese marks, and cannot always tell what is valuable or scarce. But on European marks many great volumes have been written, and there is no need I should go into them here. If you buy with a view to making your house look pretty you will avoid the European and cleave to the Oriental, and a few years hence the labours of investigators may have determined the comparative rarity and value of the pieces in your collection. As an example of the difference in value

at present between European and foreign work I may
mention the case of an eminent Parisian manufacturer
who produced at a price of forty guineas each a
pair of jars such as could be imported from China,
and sold here for forty shillings.

Of all so-called *bric-à-brac*, the highest prices are
given for early examples of Sèvres. They are seldom
beautiful, yet they deserve a certain amount of praise
as being among the few original pieces of European
work we can point out. The Sèvres decoration was its
own invention. It is not imitated from China or Japan,
though it has been imitated in all directions of late.
The colours are generally staring, but sometimes very
delicate, and the little pictures are often exquisite
examples of miniature painting. It is not, however,
for such specimens that the highest prices are given,
but for an early style of purplish pink, known as Rose
du Barry, and an equally unpleasing green, both
spotted with a kind of diaper work of feebly painted
rosebuds.

I do not think plates look well hung on the wall
They should be put on shelves in a kind of dresser.
Such a piece of furniture looks very suitable in a
dining-room, and may be made convenient as well as
pretty. China in the dining-room may consist of
plates and dishes, ranged neatly on the sideboard, but
china in the drawing-room should only consist of
purely ornamental objects and of tea things.

I have seen brown ware and Flemish grey pottery
used with good effect in a library or on a staircase.
Such pottery is very strong, and the housemaid will
seldom succeed in breaking it when she is dusting.

Some of the forms are very pretty, and the grey has the further merit that no two pieces are exactly alike. I speak here only of the original ware. In modern imitations dozens of jugs and jars are moulded to the same pattern, but such examples are valueless. You can always tell the genuine from the cast work by the marks of the mould, and by the evident tokens of original handywork in the older vessels.

Maiolica also has a very decorative effect, but it is not easy to obtain Maiolica. Time was when tourists in Italy, if they were wise, always brought some home; but now you cannot obtain anything good, and must be on your guard as to forgeries. I am frequently asked to look at so-called Maiolica and faïence which I can see at a glance is a forgery. But failing old Italian pottery there is plenty of beautiful and effective ware made in Algiers, and even in Spain, which may be picked up very cheap, and if artfully disposed in a room be made to look very pretty. Such things, however, must be carefully selected and still more carefully placed. Do not be induced to turn your rooms into a museum ; and if you place a large quantity of china or pottery on your shelves take care that some at least is bright and fresh-looking, for nothing can be more dingy than a large quantity of such things as Etruscan or Greek vases, Moorish brown and black ware, Egyptian stone bottles, and modern Norman or German grés. These are all things beautiful in themselves. They will have an excellent effect if judiciously contrasted with Japanese jars and bowls, but by themselves they only suit a great hall, or at best, the buffet of a very large dining-room.

In speaking of the objects on which the collector at home spends his admiration, I have avoided mentioning a number of things of value and beauty because they do not in the ordinary course of events come into our houses, and because it is only people of great wealth who can buy enough of them to make any great show.

Such are enamels, ivories, bronzes, marbles, jewels, and gold or silver plate. Yet it may be worth while to say a few words about them in order.

Enamels are very ornamental, very valuable in the history of art, and very indestructible. But a single picture of Limoges work, some six or seven inches square, will cost you forty, fifty, or sixty guineas, according to the period and beauty. The brilliant Japanese Cloisonné enamels are much cheaper, and have a very charming effect; they may be bought at very reasonable prices in comparison with Limoges, but they are still dearer than porcelain, though well worth the difference. If you collect such things you had better give some special study to the subject. It is a complicated and difficult one, and forgeries are common.

Ivories, generally speaking, cannot be forged. In that respect they are like illuminated MSS. An ivory carving is valued by the merit of the workmanship bestowed on it, and if the carvers could produce diptychs and triptychs like those of the middle ages, they would be nearly, if not quite, as valuable. The collector of ivories, therefore, may trust to his own

taste, if he has any, and need not fear to be taken in.
If he is taken in he deserves his fate. Imitations of
late years have been attempted of some very ancient
ivories. For the most part these are not ornamental
objects, and are chiefly of interest to the scientific
collector. It is therefore hardly necessary for me to
warn my reader that if he is offered the leaf of a con-
sular diptych of the third century he had better take
it to the British Museum or South Kensington before
he buys it.

But there can be no question about the beautiful
statuettes of the thirteenth, fourteenth, and fifteenth
centuries, which sometimes occur for sale; and I cannot
but wish our Gothic revival had directed some artist
of genius to work in ivory. Fiammingo's work, too, of
a totally different style is very pretty, and good
imitations of it are to be had. But it is safe to avoid
what is rude and what is commonplace. We see
numberless Venuses and Cupids and a few Saints in
the ivory shops, but it is seldom we find one in which
the carver has shown any knowledge of anatomy or
proportion, or has been able to give his work any
expression.

Bronzes may in many respects be classed with
ivories, except that forgeries are very common and
very deceptive. It requires special study to judge of
a good bronze, and it is not worth while to go into
the whole subject here. A separate treatise would
be required for it.

And it is much the same with plate. Within the
last few years the date marks on old gold and silver
have been carefully examined. The connoisseur can

tell easily what age a piece of silver purports to be. But electrotyping has made forgery so easy that it hardly deserves the name of forgery. The collector must judge by merit alone. There is great beauty in some styles of silver work, and it does not require much knowledge to tell the genuineness of any but rare and ancient marks. The precious metals are always worth their weight, and good workmanship, whether genuine or imitative, also counts for what it has cost.

It would be easy, indeed, to write a chapter on the silversmith's art as it is at present. The revival in painting, architecture, and many other arts does not seem to have reached the silversmith. There are few more distressing sights to the sensitive eye than a sideboard set out with yachting or racing prizes. A "cup" consists of a block of silver on which is a cast metal representation of a cutter in full sail, or a stag after Landseer, but a long way behind, or a group of ill-modelled horses and jockeys. Of chasing and *repoussé* work, as it was understood by Cellini, our designers know nothing. Their most ambitious efforts resemble the Prince Consort Memorial or a wedding-cake indifferently, and their ordinary works violate every canon of taste, and are so evidently only vehicles for the employment of so many ounces of metal that they do not come under the denomination of art in any sense.

Much the same is to be said of jewellery, but some attempts have been made of late years to improve design and setting. In such matters we are too much in the hands of professional tradesmen, and might

with advantage, when we wish to give a friend an
ornament insist on designing it for ourselves. In such
matters, however, emancipation is not easily attained.
All the power of queen, lords, and commons could
not prevent the jewellers from cutting down the koh-
i-noor, though they materially reduced its weight,
and consequently impaired its value in the process.
Nor could all the criticisms of judges, nor the ridicule
of the whole money-using public, prevent us from
having such a design as that on our florins put into
circulation and retained as English money. We can
never assert before a foreigner that as a nation we
love art, so long as he has only to take out a two-
shilling piece, or even a penny, and show us the
image and superscription. .

Stained glass is sometimes an object of pursuit
with collectors, and few things more beautiful can be
brought into a house. It is now much used for
window screens with pleasing effect. But for the most
part our modern glass fails in having too much colour,
or too many colours in one composition, and not
enough of a neutral character. Enough light cannot
be transmitted where this is the case. But sometimes
good pieces, old or new, are to be had. When a
window has to be closed permanently, which sometimes happens where there are cross lights, a black
board with holes in which specimens of glass are
inserted may be used with excellent effect. Such
a window is represented in the annexed cut. A
thorough light in a library had to be stopped, and
although the window was very large it was easily
managed by placing a great oak cupboard across

the lower half, and by hanging a picture in stained
glass framed in a black board across the upper. The
effect thus simply attained is very satisfactory.

CHAPTER V.

ART AND MORALS.

HERE seems to be something para-
doxical in talking of the cultivation of
taste as a moral duty. Yet a little
reflection may perhaps convince us, not
only that it may be a moral but even a religious duty.
Strangely enough, in the minds of most of us, music
enters largely into the idea we form of the happiness
of heaven. But why do we exclude all other kinds of
art? And if we look on the home here as the prototype
of the home hereafter, we may see reasons for making
it as a sacred thing, beautiful and pleasant, as, indeed,
we have no hesitation about making our churches.

If we follow Bishop Butler in speaking of this life
as a state of probation, and if we allow that home
life is the highest "ideal type of the life in heavenly
'mansions,'" we find ourselves forced to go a little
further, and to contemplate our own houses, our fire-
sides, our sitting rooms, our surroundings in the house,
or, in a word, all those things which go to make up

our notions of *home*, with a kind of moral and even a religious reverence.

I cannot go here into the religious topics started by the contemplation of home life, but I have said enough to show that reasons may exist for asserting that a working view of Christianity would include an ideal of heaven as a home, and help us to do something while we can to establish and increase neatness and order, beauty and sweetness, music and art, in all the houses which may come under our influence, feeling as we do so that we do something towards raising ourselves and others, and bringing heaven nearer to earth.

To make home what it should be, a cheerful, happy habitation, to which the absent members of a family may look with love, and to which the wanderer will always return with joy, we must have it not only clean, for cleanliness is next to godliness, and wholesome, which is another way of saying holy, but also beautiful. Refinement cannot go with sordidness and ugliness. Even the Scotch meeting-house is now beginning to lose its distinctive plainness. We in England have decorated our churches sometimes perhaps a little too much. And it is surely time we turned to that second church, the temple in which even the old heathen placed a family altar, and would give our homes a little more of the beauty which comes of order and purity.

Money is not what we most require for such a purpose. I have endeavoured to show this already. A pleasant and lovely home need not be expensive. To make a house beautiful we do not require gilding and carving, marble and bronze, but we do want a little taste, and perhaps a little trouble. Simplicity is not incompatible with art, even high art. It is, indeed, as we are so often taught by the art of the Greeks, and the scarcely less perfect art of our own thirteenth century, an element in true beauty, and no one can think a room less pleasant because it is furnished with studied plainness.

A pretty and pleasant house, whether in town or country, is a centre of life radiating into other houses. If a house in a London street shows signs of being cared for and well treated, other houses soon begin to look like it. Art is very infectious in such things. Taste spreads with wonderful rapidity. Thirty years ago if you asked schoolboys or young ladies about their knowledge of architecture they would probably have repeated the names of the five classical orders, and there would have begun and ended their information. Now every church, almost every school, in our land shows signs of the knowledge and taste in Gothic and Elizabethan art of young curates and rectors' daughters. It is high time something of the kind should spread to our dwelling-houses. How many young ladies now spend their time making minute water-colour sketches while their father has to bring in a house-painter to "do up" a sitting-room. Yet there is no reason I can think of why a young lady should not paint and decorate a door as easily as she paints a view in the Highlands or a fisherman's family. If the complete decoration of a room would be too much, all the details, not only the carving of mouldings, and the colouring of panels, but even the arrangement of a tile pattern and the design of a window leading might be done at home.

One house in which the inmates set themselves from their first coming to do nothing except in good taste would soon become a centre of civilisation in a country district. Nothing will keep the boys at home of an evening more certainly than a little art, whether music or painting. The sons of a family in moments of leisure could carve a chimney-piece which would be a credit to the country at large. The trouble spent in learning a quartet would be perhaps just as well, certainly no worse, spent in learning to paint a motto over the door. It requires no greater exertion to make an embroidered curtain or *portière* than to make a dozen "anti-macassars." What is chiefly wanted for such ambitious efforts is a little taste and knowledge, and the schools of art all through the country might supply both if they would. So far they have done very little for the improvement of home art. Perhaps the school water-colours are a little less hard and impossible. Perhaps a few students have learned enough figure drawing not to make the men and women in their sketches look so like jointed dolls. But very little has yet been done to give people rules how to draw and stencil a diaper all over a bedroom wall, how to choose two delicate colours for the panels of a cupboard, or how to make a plaster work pattern for the drawing-room ceiling. This is what the local schools have yet to do, what some sanguine people imagined they would do, and what they never will do under South Kensington management as it is at present.

To prove that I am not expecting too much, I have only to point to cases like that one at Lambeth, in which a school of art becoming connected with the practical art of a pottery, has produced some of the best work we have had in England for five hundred years.

Drawing classes and clubs sensibly conducted might do much for the improvement of art at home, but, so far as they have hitherto been tried, they have usually degenerated into parties for the cultivation of the art of flirting, and if I recommend that the sexes study drawing apart I lay myself open to the answer that under such conditions the sexes will prefer not to study drawing at all. In any case a good teacher is one of the first requisites and one generally done without. The second thing required is subordination, which of all virtues is the one most often wanting among amateurs. A class well conducted and well organized might undertake the painting and decoration of a village school, or a mechanics' institute, but the difficulty would of course be double. It would be necessary for every one to work under the direction of one master-mind, and for such a master-mind to be found.

The village is very small in which during the winter something of the nature of penny readings is not held. At penny readings, lectures, and especially illustrated lectures on art, might be given with advantage. Few clergymen are without some knowledge of architecture. Few intelligent men, in fact, are without some special knowledge of one branch of art or another. It is very easy to get such people to give short

lectures. People would not be tired by a quarter of
an hour on the structure of a flying buttress, or the
life of Reynolds, or the frescoes in the Campo Santo
at Pisa, or the meaning of Dürer's *Melencholia*, or the
Japanese way of drawing foliage. I do not speak
without some experience of the subject. I have seen
a large audience composed chiefly of working men in
a mining district very much interested by a series
of short lectures on architecture, delivered as part of
the entertainments of an evening. A few diagrams
are necessary, but they are easily made, and few
places are without an amateur able to draw them.

The civilising influence of art has been matter of
remark since the time of Ovid at least, and it is high
time in these days of culture that we should try its
virtue. We talk too much about these things and do
too little. The smallest child in the village school
learns singing, but no child learns drawing. Yet of
the two—singing and drawing—which is the most
likely to be of use in after life? It is objected
perhaps, that all children have not a taste for drawing,
but neither have all children a taste for music, as we
have full proof every Sunday in church, at least. A
more serious objection is that masters and mistresses
have already too many "subjects," and cannot make
them all equally familiar. But the thing might at
least be tried, and I think it would soon be found that
an amateur would turn up to solve the difficulty in a
great many places, just as at present the village choir
is often trained by voluntary labour.

But it is more among adults than children that the
beneficial influence of art may be seen. In small

country towns and villages it is sometimes not easy to get so many performers together as will constitute a band, but a class for art study, for drawing, or carving, would not require any particular number. No matter how small the village, the public-house finds no difficulty in keeping full; and there is nothing so efficacious in counteracting the public-house as a little cultivation. It is ridiculous to lecture on temperance and force total abstinence on hard-worked men, unless you often find them some compensating entertainment, and I hope and believe that before very long this truth will be recognized, and some artistic object of interest for evening entertainment be added to the few now existing to counteract the tavern. The longing for beauty is acknowledged by the tavern-keepers. They are obliged to supply the want. They have music if possible, and the grog shop is transformed into a palace. Marble and granite columns, carved oak stalls, shining glass and silver, coloured lights and mirrors, are lavishly spent to attract the workman. If such an outlay pays, and it must pay or it would not be incurred so frequently, we may feel perfectly sure that the "licensed victualler" has hit on a want and supplies it. All these scenic and architectural effects are produced because he knows that the people whose lives are spent in labour have a craving for the sight of what is beautiful, and that if they can resist the mere attraction of drinking by itself, they will not be able to resist it when it is backed up and helped by all the gorgeous surroundings of the gin palace.

A movement has of late years been made at the

east end of London to do something to mitigate the sordid ugliness of home life. That working people should care for art or should like to see pretty things was thought a short time ago perfectly ridiculous. Their houses were miserable and filthy, and they showed no taste either in their dress, or in their personal habits. One of the first moves was made by a parochial exhibition of works of art, which was held in one or two places. The people brought some curious specimens of domestic manufacture. Old samplers, full rigged ships in fish-bone, cardboard models, a few drawings, a black letter family Bible or two, an old German engraving—many such objects were shown, and the interest excited was very great. Then came the Bethnal Green Museum. To everybody's surprise the people flocked there in crowds, and competent witnesses declared that the working man's remarks on pictures were often at least as sensible as those of some professed critics.

It will be a great pity if this movement is allowed to die out. Mr. Harry Jones has got leave to make a garden of the dreary waste of tombs which surrounds St. George's-in-the-East, and some benevolent ladies are endeavouring to start a " Beauty Mission " for the homes of the people, and I heartily wish them success. A few bare walls hung with pictures, a few flowers in the windows, a pretty tile on the hob, would, in my opinion, do more to keep men and women at home, and to promote family love, than libraries of tracts and platforms full of temperance lecturers.

While we thus think of the homes of the poor, it

will not do for us to neglect our own. Mothers wonder oftentimes that their sons care so little for staying at home. But does it occur to them to ask themselves what they have done to make home happy and pleasant ? not happy only but pleasant also. Even a merry house, if it is untidy and dirty, if it is dingy and ugly, is unattractive to young people. They are unconsciously very sensitive to external impressions. The comfort and good taste of the club drawing-room has as much to do as the company and newspapers in bringing young men from home. Our sons are literally driven out to seek away from home that comfort and order which is there denied them. We nip the youthful taste in the bud : we look on mere art as a useless expense, and we lose hold of the strongest cord by which we might bind our children to home.

A wise father—all whose children have turned out well, and in different places and employments still love their home—told me that he encouraged each of them from the first to "make a collection." Some of them had more decided taste than others. To several postage stamps and such insipid objects were enough. Others preferred pictures, engravings, carvings, or something distinctly artistic. In after life all these young men and women found themselves in the possession of at least a portion of the pocket-money they had received in youth, and found themselves moreover possessed of that inestimable advantage, whether in a busy or in an idle life, a love for something which would serve as an amusement and relaxation for leisure hours.

Such people have no occasion for card-playing or gambling to pass a long evening. To them a spare hour is not an enemy to be killed. Satan finds no mischief for their idle hands to do. They wonder how anyone can complain of *ennui*, for their time is fully occupied, and life is only too short for what they want to get into it.

So, too, even their passive enjoyment is immensely increased. The taste for fine scenery is a modern invention, and assuredly it is one of the greatest benefits mankind has received. I cannot help thinking our modern love of beautiful landscape is the sign of a general improvement of all our race. Mankind has not been able till within the last few centuries to see fully how beautiful nature is, and now the love of nature is like a sixth sense. Virgil and the classical poets only introduce landscape incidentally. The Christian poets, with King David himself to lead them, alone describe natural loveliness properly— that is, religiously.

There is a yearning towards beauty in form and colour as well as in sound and in morals: and this yearning has almost always taken a religious direction. Even the impure worship of the Grecian gods had its pure æsthetic side : and the neglected author of the Book of Wisdom points it out in words worthy to be remembered :—" The sky is fair," he says, " but He that made it fairer; " and he counsels those who love Nature to look beyond it, observing that they "deemed neither fire or wind or the swift air, or the circle of the stars, or the violent water, or the lights of heaven, to be the gods which govern the world; with whose beauty if they being delighted took them to be gods, let them know how much better the Lord of them is : for the first author of beauty hath created them." And St. Augustine expresses the same thought or one like it, and with almost equal majesty.

It is to this upward yearning of men's minds that the wise educator will address himself. The higher our conception of material beauty, the higher will be our ideal of moral beauty. The more we study nature the more complex, the more complete she appears. The higher we rise in our intellectual progress, the further does wisdom seem to soar above us. And as day by day, year by year, age by age, we enlarge our power of conceiving beauty and harmony, the more beautiful, the more harmonious does Creation appear to us. "Man doth seek," says an old writer,[1] "a triple perfection. First, a sensual, consisting in those things which very life itself requireth, either as necessary supplements or as beauties and ornaments thereof. Then an intellectual, consisting of those things which none underneath man is either capable of or acquainted with. Lastly, a spiritual or divine consisting in those things whereunto we tend by supernatural means here, but here cannot attain unto them." And again, a little further on, "although the beauties, riches, honours, sciences, virtues, and perfections of all men living were in the present possession of one : yet somewhat above and beyond all this there would still be sought and earnestly thirsted for. So that Nature, even in this life, doth plainly claim and call for a more divine perfection."

[1] Hooker, *Eccl. Pol.*, B. i. 35.

What this perfection is, how we shall know it, not even Hooker could tell us. To some it may appear in one way, to others in another. It may come to us at home in the monotonous round of duty: it may be like a vision of angels by a stony pillow in a foreign land: or it may be reserved for that hereafter in which we shall recognise without doubt the author of all moral and material beauty, and know openly the features which here perchance we have often passed by in the crowd.

LONDON :

R   CLAY, SONS, AND TAYLOR, PRINTERS,

COLLINSON & LOCK.

ARTISTIC FURNITURE IN THE OLD ENGLISH STYLE.

Inexpensive.
Soundly constructed.
Most finished workmanship.

CONSTRUCTIVE WOODWORK FOR INTERIORS.

Staircases, Wall Panelling,
Ceilings, Windows,
Mantel-Pieces, and Doors.

CURTAIN FABRICS OF SILK, WOOL, AND COTTON.

Of Special Design
and Colour.
Reproductions of Old Brocades.

DECORATIVE WALL AND CEILING PAPERS.

109, FLEET STREET,
LONDON, E.C.

ART AT HOME SERIES.

A Plea for Art in the House. With Special Reference . to the Economy of Collecting Works of Art, and the Importance of Taste in Education and Morals. By W. J. LOFTIE, B.A., F.S.A., Author of "In and Out of London." With Illustrations, Crown 8vo. 2s. 6d. [*Ready.*

Suggestions for House Decoration in Painting, Woodwork, and Furniture. By RHODA and AGNES GARRETT. With Illustrations, Crown 8vo, 2s. 6d. [*Ready.*

Drawing and Painting. By H. STACEY MARKS, A.R.A.

Dress. By MRS. OLIPHANT.

Family Music. By JOHN HULLAH.

Domestic Architecture. By J. J. STEVENSON.

Other Vols. on Gardening, Sculpture and Carving, Needlework and Lace-making, and other Subjects connected with Art at Home, will follow.

MACMILLAN AND CO., LONDON.

www.ingramcontent.com/pod-product-compliance
Lightning Source LLC
Chambersburg PA
CBHW032148010726
47493CB00008BA/2631